DISCARD

SMALL *Oxford* BOOKS

CYCLING

SMALL *Oxford* BOOKS

CYCLING

Compiled by
JEANNE MACKENZIE

Oxford New York Toronto Melbourne
OXFORD UNIVERSITY PRESS
1981

Oxford University Press, Walton Street, Oxford OX2 6DP

London Glasgow New York Toronto
Delhi Bombay Calcutta Madras Karachi
Kuala Lumpur Singapore Hong Kong Tokyo
Nairobi Dar es Salaam Cape Town
Melbourne Wellington

and associate companies in
Beirut Berlin Ibadan Mexico City

British Library Cataloguing in Publication Data

Cycling – (Small Oxford books)
1. Cycling – Literary collections
I. MacKenzie, Jeanne
809'.93355   PN6071.C95   80-42095
ISBN 0-19-214117-1

Printed in Great Britain by
Hazell Watson & Viney Limited
Aylesbury, Bucks

Introduction

The bicycle got off to a slow start. For a long time it was no more than an idea and a dream. Leonardo da Vinci saw the potentiality of movement and his drawings show a bicycle-like machine. Throughout the seventeenth century people experimented with carriages propelled by legs instead of horses but they were not very practical. In 1790 an eccentric Parisian, Monsieur de Sivrac, rode a wooden horse's body on four wheels; it was called the *celérifère*, then renamed the *velocifère*. This comical and limited device was taken up by the fashionable youth of Paris and races were held in the Champs-Élysées. Then, in 1818, Paris was taken with an even more ingenious machine invented by a German engineer, Baron Karl von Drais. He removed the horse's head and body, made the front wheel pivot so that it could be steered round corners, and put a pad on the front of the frame which enabled the rider to lean forward to get the maximum impetus. News of this Draisienne, or velocipede, soon spread to England and for a time it was a fashionable pastime.

It was not until the 1840s that any significant progress was made, when a blacksmith called Kirkpatrick Macmillan redesigned the hobby horse to give it two pedals attached by connecting rods to arms on the back wheel. He also introduced a brake. Now, for the first time, the rider had both feet off the ground: it was the beginning of the modern bicycle. By the time of the great Exhibition of 1851 there were three velocipedes on show and such machines were soon on sale.

The way was now open for all kinds of designs – with four wheels, or one, driven by the feet, or by hand. Into this variety came the 'bone-shaker' from France. It came from the workshop of Pierre Michaux, near the Champs-Élysées. With his sons and a colleague, Michaux devised a crank to fit to the front wheel of machines adapted from the old Draisienne. The contrivance was called a *bicircle* or *veloce*. When he introduced the machine at the Paris Exhibition of 1867 the public took to it at once. Velocipedes, although expensive, became the rage.

The Franco-Prussian War brought an end to all such frivolity in France but the new machine caught on in America. The bicycle was everywhere, on the stage, in music-halls, in acrobatics, and on the streets. Blondin pedalled his bone-shaker across Niagara Falls on a wire. But it was no more than a passing craze. 'Sliding down hill on a handsaw, tooth side up,' one writer declared, 'would be two degrees more comfortable than experimenting on one of these contrivances.'

In England the bone-shaker fared better. In 1868 the Paris agent of the Coventry Sewing Machine Company, Rowley Turner, was so taken by the Michaux machines that he took one to England and by February 1869 his company was in production under the name of the Coventry Machinist Company. The general foreman of the firm, James Starley, was an inventive genius and he turned his ingenuity to making the Michaux lighter and easier to handle. It caused quite a stir when it appeared on the streets – 'them queer horses', 'whirligigs', 'menageries' and 'valparaisos' were some of the cranky names it acquired. But for all the gibes the bicycle caught on and there were soon cycling clubs and organized races for enthusiasts.

The bone-shaker had started a craze but all the time ingenious mechanics were trying to design a lighter and faster machine. One way to cover more ground with each stroke of the pedal was to increase the size of the front wheel. In 1870 James Starley produced a bicycle called the 'ariel' in which the front wheel was 50 inches in diameter and the back was a mere 14 inches, with the rider precariously balanced over the front wheel. A year later this all-metal bicycle was in production and sold for between £8 and £12. It became known as the Ordinary bicycle and later, just because of its odd-sized wheels, it was nicknamed the Penny Farthing. The bicycle was now becoming a common sight and by the mid-1870s there were 50,000 high-wheelers on the roads. The Ordinary was fun, and it was also relatively efficient. There were races, stunts, competitions. For all the jokes about 'cads on castors' and 'monkeys on wires' the bicycle had to be reckoned with. 'Bicyclists have become a power' declared *The Times*. In 1878 the Bicycle Union was formed and before long it became the Cyclists Touring Club.

There was, however, one real snag. The Ordinary was hard to manage and far from safe. There was a real danger of falling forward: it was such a common mishap that it acquired a distinctive name of 'header', 'cropper', or 'imperial crowner'. In any case such a machine was really more suited to athletes and Bohemian youth, as Starley discovered when he vainly tried to adapt it for ladies by making a side saddle. The tricycle was a more popular solution and by the late Seventies there were dozens of different designs on the market. Starley produced the 'Sociable' on which two cyclists could ride side by side, and it was while out riding this machine with his son that he hit upon a vital change in design. He devised the differential gear which enabled the wheels to rotate independently and thus prevent the machine from veering all over the road. The result was the 'Salvo Quod' which became the 'Royal Salvo' when Queen Victoria ordered two of them in 1881. Tricycling was now taken up by the aristocracy, the gentry and even ladies – who were soon to find that the new gadget would change their costume and their whole way of life.

How to produce a machine that was safe? Attempts to solve that pressing problem led to all kinds of experiments. There was the back-to-front Ordinary with the little wheel at the front; there were others with names like the 'Xtraordinary', the 'Facile', and the 'Kangaroo'. For all their claims to be safe from headers and side falls, none of them was really satisfactory. Then in 1885 Starley's nephew, John Kemp Starley, produced the Rover 'safety' bicycle driven by a chain to the back wheel with wheels of equal and smaller size. It established a new 100 mile record of 7 hours 5 minutes and 16 seconds. Its success was instantaneous. It was produced in eight different models at a cost from under £10, and by 1890 dozens of small manufacturers were producing a safety bicycle like the Rover.

This great change was soon consolidated by another technical improvement. In July 1888 John Boyd Dunlop, a veterinary surgeon in Belfast, patented a pneumatic tyre. The way was now clear for the modern safety bicycle. In 1895 over 800,000 cycles were produced in England. The bicycle had changed from a fad to a welcome convenience and a democratic source of pleasure. Now every man was king of the road and every woman a queen.

'I think I shall always stick to my bike', said Christopher. 'The bicycle is the most civilized conveyance known to man. Other forms of transport grow daily more nightmarish. Only the bicycle remains pure in heart.'

Iris Murdoch, *The Red and the Green*, 1965

The Nothing of the Day

In 1768 James Boswell recorded this conversation about one of the earliest experiments to make a bicycle:

There was a pretty large circle this evening. Dr. Johnson was in very good humour, lively, and ready to talk upon all subjects. Mr. Ferguson, the astronomer, told him of a new-invented machine which went without horses. A man who sat in it turned a handle which worked a spring that drove it forward. 'Then, Sir,' said Johnson, 'what is gained is, the man has his choice whether he will move himself alone, or himself and the machine too.'

26 October 1768, James Boswell, *Life of Samuel Johnson*

Early in 1819 a coachmaker at Covent Garden called Dennis Johnson patented his version of the German Draisienne, a two-wheeled machine which was already popular in Paris. In February John Keats wrote to George and Georgiana Keats:

The nothing of the day is a machine called the Velocipede. It is a wheel-carriage to ride cock horse upon, sitting astride and pushing it along with the toes, a rudder wheel in hand. They will go seven miles an hour. A handsome gelding will come to eight guineas, however they will soon be cheaper, unless the army takes to them.

Collected Letters

Variants of the device soon appeared.

The Duke and Duchess of Kent ... Tuesday, at five o'clock, upon their return to Kensington Palace, their Royal Highnesses had chairs, and sat on the walk at the east front of the Palace, when Mr Birch, the coach-maker, exhibited to them a curious constructed vehicle, called the Velocimanipede, or Phaeton in Miniature, calculated to carry three persons. The centre, or body of the carriage, is supposed to be for a female; the front is for a gentleman to sit on a narrow saddle to guide it. At the back is a small dickey to work the hind wheels by machinery. Their Royal Highnesses expressed their gratification at the ingenious contrivance . . . .

Morning Chronicle, 13 May 1819

The velocipede caught on with the swells and dandies of the day. Although Cruikshank and Gillray used it to make fun of the Prince Regent and the aristocracy, there were some who had a sense of happy, free-wheeling days to come.

A dandy, on a velocipede,
I saw in a vision sweet,
Along the highway making speed,
With his alternate feet.
Of a bright and celestial hue,
Gleam'd beauteously his blue surtout;
While ivory buttons, in a row,
Showed like the winter's cavern'd snow,
Which the breezy North
Drives sweeping forth,
To lodge in the cave below:
Ontario's beaver, without demur,
To form his hat did lend its fur:
His frill was of the cambric fine,
And his neckcloth starch'd and aquiline;
And oh, the eye with pleasure dwells
On his white jean indescribables:
And he throws the locks from his forehead fair,
And he pants, and pants, and pants for air.

Blackwoods Magazine, May 1821

Though some perhaps will me despise,
Others my charms will highly prize
Yet, nevertheless, think themselves wise.
Sometimes, 'tis true, I am a toy,
Contrived to please some active boy;
But I amuse each Jack O'Dandy,
E'en great men sometimes have me handy,
Who, when on me get astride
Think that on Pegasus they ride.

Anon.

Even this simple machine found its way to America.

Some of the Harvard College students who boarded in my neighbourhood had these machines, then called velocipedes, on which they used to waddle along like so many ducks, their feet pushing against the ground, and looking as if they were perched on portable treadmills. They soon found that legs were made before velocipedes.

Oliver Wendell Holmes, *The Autocrat of the Breakfast-Table*,
1858

VELOCIPEDOMANIA

A machine that was recognizable as a bicycle came into being in the early 1840s when for the first time the rider had both feet off the ground, and in the 1860s 'the bone-shaker' made its appearance in France.

The velocoman, as he styles himself, is to be seen in all his glory, careering at full speed through the shady avenues of the Bois de Boulogne or skimming like some gigantic dragonfly over the level surface of the roads intersecting the Champs-Élysées.

Girl of the Period Miscellany, May 1869

Paris is just now afflicted with a serious nuisance ... velocipedes, machines like the ghosts of departed spiders, on which horrible boys and detestable men career about the streets and boulevards. ... The Parisians scarcely know whether to scowl or to laugh at this new outrage.

Once a Week, 21 March 1868

Some scowled.

Velocipedists are imbeciles on wheels.

Le Gaulois, 17 February 1869

Even so, the craze caught on in America and in England.

The art of walking is obsolete. It is true that a few still cling to that mode of locomotion, are still admired as fossil specimens of an extinct race of pedestrians, but for the majority of civilized humanity, walking is on its last legs.

Scientific American, 9 January 1869

The two wheeled velocipede is the animal which is to supersede everything else. It costs but little to produce, and still less to keep. It does not eat cart loads of hay, and does not wax fat and kick. It is easy to handle. It never rears up. It won't bite. It needs no check or rein or halter, or any unnatural restraint. It is little and light, let alone it will lean lovingly against the nearest support. It never flies off at a tangent unless badly managed, and under no circumstances will it shy at anything.

The Velocipedist, 1869

Entertainers were quick to see its possibilities and the velocipede was used in stunts both on and off the stage.

21 June 1869. To Fenchurch Street, and went down by rail to North Woolwich ... I went into the 'Royal Gardens'.... In a large hall or ballroom in the grounds,

VELOCIPEDES.
WOOD BROTHERS,
                    596 Broadway, New York,

a farce, a concert, a ballet, went on successively. . . .
Then the hall was cleared, everyone standing around it;
a couple of the new two-wheeled velocipedes were
brought in; and the 'French Female Velocipedists'
appeared: Two girls of 18 or 20, one of them very
pretty, and both well made and graceful. They were
drest as men; in jockey caps, and satin jackets and
short breeches ending above the knee, and long
stockings, and mid-length boots. Thus clad, they
stepped forth unabashed into the midst, and mounted
their 'bicycles'; each girl throwing her leg over and
sitting astride on the saddle. And then they started,
amidst cheers; pursuing one another round and round
the hall, curving in and out, sometimes rising in their
stirrups (so to speak) as if trotting, sometimes throwing
one leg or both legs up whilst at full speed: and after
riding so, with the skill and vigour of young men, for a
quarter of an hour, these girls halted and dismounted,
and made their bow amidst thunder of applause.
'They're fine made girls', said a respectable matron

near me: and the man who had charge of their steeds observed, 'They've got some English velocipede-girls at Cremorne, as rides astride like these here; but lor, they can't hold a candle to these two!' It seems that the fair cavaliers are circus riders from the Paris Hippodrome, not unused, therefore, to bestriding a horse. . . . There was nothing indecent in the performance, or in the girls' behaviour; if once you grant that a woman may, like a man, wear breeches and sit astride in public.

Derek Hudson, *Munby, Man of Two Worlds: Life and Diaries of Arthur J. Munby 1828–1910*, 1972

For all its advantages riding a bone-shaker was no easy matter. The Reverend G. Herbert recalled riding a velocipede in Cambridge in the 1870s:

The wheels were nearly of a size, about 36 inches high; the felloes were of iron, flat like those of a waggon; there were no rubber tyres, and though to us then it seemed to go with the greatest of ease, it made a mighty rattle, needing no warning bell to tell the unwary pedestrian of its approach . . . mounting was the worst part of the whole process. . . . Grasping the handles, we set off at a fast run, keeping alongside the machine till we got considerable momentum on it, then we vaulted into the saddle. This required practice and agility. . . . After sundry scratches, many bruises . . . I at last mastered the art. . . . Of course these early machines were merely toys, for we used to think eleven or twelve miles a good ride. The labour was considerable and the chafing excessive. A railway bridge or a very slight rise in the ground brought us to a standstill.

Arnold Bennett gave it a place in literature.

One morning in March, a boneshaker . . . disturbed the gravity of St Luke's Square. . . . The boneshaker was brought forth by Dick Povey, the only son of Daniel, now aged eleven years, under the superintendence of his father, and the Square soon perceived that Dick had a natural talent for breaking in an untrained bone-shaker. After a few attempts he could remain on the back of the machine for at least ten yards, and his feat had the effect of endowing St Luke's Square with the attractiveness of a circus. . . . Presently Daniel Povey and Dick went to the top of the Square with the machine . . . and Dick, being carefully installed in the saddle, essayed to descend the gentle paven slopes of the Square. He failed time after time; the machine had an astonishing way of turning round, running uphill, and then lying calmly on its side. . . . At last the boneshaker was displaying less unwillingness to obey, and lo! in a moment Dick was riding down the Square, and the spectators held their breath as if he had been Blondin crossing Niagara. Every second he ought to have fallen off, but he contrived to keep upright. Already he had accomplished twenty yards – thirty yards! It was a miracle that he was performing! . . . Yes, he would arrive; he would do it! . . . And the intrepid child surged on, and, finally victorious, crashed into the pavement . . . at the rate of quite six miles an hour. . . . 'Not so bad for a start, eh?' exclaimed the great Daniel.

The Old Wives Tale, 1908

The bone-shaker had its drawbacks, for all its success.

Bicycle riding, if gone in for to any great extent, results in depression, in exhaustion and in wear and tear. . . . Unless anyone is possessed of legs of iron and thighs of brass, I would strongly recommend him to look before he leaps into the saddle of a bicycle.

English Mechanic, 17 September 1869

CADS ON CASTORS

The result of experiments to make the bicycle lighter and faster was the Ordinary – later known as the Penny Farthing – in which the front wheel was more than three times the size of the back with the rider precariously balanced over the front wheel. It was no easy machine to ride.

Mine was not a full-grown bicycle, but only a colt – a fifty inch, with the pedals shortened up to forty-eight – and skittish, like any other colt. The Expert explained the thing's points briefly, then he got on its back and rode around a little, to show me how easy it was to do. He said that dismounting was perhaps the hardest thing to learn, and so we would leave that to the last. But, he was in error there. He found, to his surprise and joy, that all he needed to do was to get me on the machine and stand out of the way: I could get off myself. Although I was wholly inexperienced, I dismounted in the best time on record. He was on that side shoving up the machine; we all came down with a crash, he at the bottom, I next, and the machine on top. . . .

Then he limped out to a position, and we resumed once more. This time the Expert took up the position of shortstop, and got a man to shove up behind. We got up a handsome speed and presently traversed a brick, and I went out over the top of the tiller and landed, head down, on the instructor's back, and saw the machine fluttering in the air between me and the sun. It was well it came down on us, for that broke the fall, and it was not injured.

Five days later I got out and was carried down to the hospital and found the Expert doing pretty fairly. In a few more days I was quite sound. . . . During eight days I took a daily lesson of an hour and a half. At the end of this twelve working-hours' apprenticeship I was graduated – in the rough. I was pronounced competent to pedal my own bicycle without outside help. . . . Before taking final leave of me, my instructor inquired concerning my physical strength, and I was able to inform him that I hadn't any. . . . Then he left me, and I started out alone to seek adventures. You don't really have to seek them – that is nothing but a phrase – they come to you. . . . It took time to learn to miss a dog, but I achieved even that. . . . Get a bicycle. You will not regret it if you live.

Mark Twain, *What is Man?*, 1906

The bicycle is a two-legged velocipede. One leg is in front and is quite sizeable; the other is behind and is very diminutive. The daring gymnast mounts the foreleg – not the leg itself, but the supposed seat, about the size of a man's hand, fixed thereon. This instrument will go unparalleled distances in any amount of time. The worst feature of the beast is that you have to get off when you go uphill; coming downhill it is warranted to kill nine and three-sixteenths times out of ten; and on level ground, it is harder work to keep the thing going than it is to walk. Many people, therefore, may fail to see where its special utility comes in.

The Columbiad, 1881

For pedestrians, the Ordinary was just as alarming.

How fast those new bicycles travelled and how dangerous they looked! Pedestrians backed almost into the hedges when they met one of them . . . it was thrilling to see a man hurtling through space on one high wheel, with another tiny wheel wobbling helplessly behind.

Flora Thompson, *Over to Candleford*, 1941

But sometimes there was a happy ending.

> A little girl with eyes of blue;
> A little dog of snowy hue;
> A little wheel, with rider rash;
> A bark, a rush, an awful crash!
>
> A little scream, a little swear;
> A pretty sympathetic air;
> A little conversation leading
> To blushes, smiles, successful pleading.
>
> A little church; a little bride;
> A gallant wheelman by her side;
> A little kiss, their vows to seal;
> A little rival for the wheel.
>
> 'A Bicycling Idyll', *Cycling*, April 1881

There were other hazards, too, for the cyclist.

Horses, it must be admitted, do not like bicycles.

The Times, 5 September 1878

If a horse, on meeting a bicycle, shows signs of restive-
ness, it is not always wise to dismount at once. To dismount suddenly is more likely to frighten a horse than
to continue riding slowly by *talking to the horse as you
do so.*

Rules of the Cambridge University Bicycle Club, 1876

Poor yellow-breasted little thing,
I would thou had'st been on the wing,
'Ere 'twas my fate on thee to bring
  Thy death so soon;
Thou'lt never more be heard to sing
  In joyful tune.

Too late I saw thee 'mongst the dust,
Gambling so gay in simple trust,
I knew that with my wheel I must
  Thy life destroy:
How cruel quick my rubber crushed
  Thee in thy joy.

From 'To a Yellow Hammer', 1881. Anon.

*For all the dangers, the Ordinary had a devoted following.
Cycling clubs were formed all over the country. Here is
how one of them began.*

I strolled one Sunday evening into a Pub called the
Admiral Nelson. . . . There were Hard working men
Spending their hard earned money in Exsesive Drink-
ing. . . .

At that time Bicycling was all the Rage. I asked these
men if they would assist me in Starting a Cycle Club
so that we could Roam instead of sitting Here drinking.
Without demanding any more Details, it was Done. We
paid half a crown each, per week. When £8 was put
together a Draw took Place and the Owner who picked
the Right Number had the First Machine. The
Manufacturer, Mr Godley of Northampton, provided

machines for men to Learn on. That so Delighted them that in a few weeks many had purchased their own. In twelve months we Paid to the Waterloo House 105 pounds for uniforms. That club grew to 185 members. When I left Northampton in 1880 I was made Captain against my will. For that Robbed me of a few hours Poaching. But I accepted that Proud Position and when I left I was Presented with a Beautiful Time-Piece which reminds me of the Pleasant Days during five years of the Rovers Bicycle Club. . . . You would have been surprised to see the Change in these men. They gained a Greater Respect for themselves, their Wives and their familys. . . .

I returned to Leicester in 1880 and left Poaching for a while. Again my attention was Drawn to Cycling. Riding at this Period was all the go . . . the People of Leicester nearly went mad with Excitement. We had in Leicester two Champions of the world on the Tall Machine . . . and for some time Leicester was Kept alive by the performances of these Cracks. They defeated all comers.

James Hawker (1836–1921),
A Victorian Poacher, 1961

In 1889 Hilaire Belloc went to France as the cycling correspondent of the Pall Mall Gazette. *He bought a new bicycle for the purpose – a 'Rapid' :*

This beats any other bicycle of the Ordinary or high type that I have ridden. Whether this is because of the large hind wheel, of the saddle adjustment, or of the tangential spokes, I do not know; but certainly no other machine with which I am acquainted gets one up to the top so easily and runs so smoothly.

From Robert Speaight, *Hilaire Belloc*, 1957

'OH, THAT TRICYCLE'

A British tricycler named Cholmondely
Once wooed a tricycleress colmondely
She frowned on his suit
And told him to scoot
Which reply he received glolmondely.

Wheeling Annual, 1881

From the beginning tricyclists set themselves apart.

Mechanics, day-labourers, chimney-sweeps, costers etc who are now hailed as men and brothers in bicycle contests, shall never find a place in the Tricycle Association.

Correspondent in *Bicycling News*, 31 May 1878

When Queen Victoria ordered two of the newest tricycles in June 1881 they quickly gained popularity with the gentry. Cycling even became a family affair for the middle classes.

My mother had (I believe) the first female tricycle in Cambridge; and I had a little one, and we used to go out for family rides, all together; my father in front on a bicycle, and poor Charles standing miserably on the bar behind my mother, holding on for all he was worth. I found it very hard work, pounding away on my hard tyres, a glorious but not a pleasurable pastime.

Gwen Raverat, *Period Piece*, 1952

It was on my seventh or eighth birthday that [my father] gave me a tricycle . . . he and my elder brother, Herbert, already each had their tricycle. On Sunday we all three set off together on our tricycles from Lexham Gardens, along the Hammersmith Road, across the bridge to Barnes Common, to Sheen and Richmond Park. In those days, after the Castelnau Road you were practically in the country. It seems to me that it was a pretty long ride for a child of seven or eight who had not often been on a tricycle before. But, as it was afterwards discovered, there was something wrong in the bottom bracket of my new tricycle and I had simply to pound along using a good deal of force to make the beastly thing go at all. I can still remember the agony of grinding along the Sheen Road on the way back, the pain of exhaustion made worse by the disappointment in the present which I had so eagerly looked forward to. I managed to conceal my condition from father and Herbert, but when we got back to Lexham Gardens, we were met at the door by my mother, anxious to know whether we had enjoyed ourselves. . . . In the hall I collapsed and was carried away and put to bed.

Leonard Woolf, *Sowing*, 1960

The tricycle gave a measure of freedom to women.

A tricycling the ladies go,
And oh, how fine they feel!
What matters it to them, although
The weary husband down at heel,
Is praying for a good square meal,
Or that at home the babies squeal
Or wallow in their weltering woe?
This is the year for hens to crow;
It is the rule, there's no appeal –
And woman's at the wheel!

Wheeling Annual, 1884

There was, however, still a problem of safety.

I tumbled out of my tricycle the other day and it shook me pretty badly. . . . My Stars and Stripes! how stiff my whole right leg is, even now.

Ellen Terry to G. B. Shaw, 9 May 1897
From *A Correspondence*, 1949

Oh, that tricycle, that tricycle! I told you that it was a dangerous contrivance; but you would have it that it was safe because it stands by itself like a perambulator when you're not on it. . . . You should see the appalling accidents we have all lived through here. . . . On trikes we'd have been slain.

> G. B. Shaw to Ellen Terry, 11 May 1897
> From *Collected Letters of G. B. Shaw,* 1965

Suddenly we heard a cry of alarm. I raised my bemused head, and saw a stout woman on a tricycle, tearing down the hill with her feet off the pedals, which were flickering up and down, as it seemed, faster than the eye could follow. An instant later there was another cry from the stout woman, and a crash alongside us. . . . Machines and human bodies appeared immediately to multiply, and to be scattered all about us, amid a cloud of white dust, and groans and cries. . . .

Father strode over to the mound of humanity in the middle of the road, lifted her up as though she were merely an inflated balloon, and assisted her to the side of the road . . . .

'Now, Ma'am!' he cried. 'Is nobody with you?' She was still incoherent, but we could detect references to her poor husband, and demands for the police, and denunciations of that monster of ungallant depravity who had brought her to this pretty pass. 'It's nobody's fault', said Father, brushing away at her garments and flicking her face and hands with her own handkerchief. 'You lost control. Should never do that, you know. Might have ruined your machine.'

By this time the poor husband approached down the hill on a bicycle of rare vintage, the back wheel being about two-thirds the size of the front one, and the chain encased in a honey-coloured, transparent gearcase square at both ends. The handlebars towered up, with grips of cork at least six inches long.

He was a small, nervous man, and he looked at my father beseechingly like a spaniel.

'I will take charge', he said. Though that was unbelievable, we left him and his runaway spouse, remounted and rode on.

Richard Church, Over the Bridge, 1955

For some the tricycle was one way of graduating to a bicycle.

> One Autumn eve, when, sharp and chill,
> The wind blew like an icicle,
> I met, fast speeding o'er the hill,
> A youth upon a bicycle.
>
> 'How glorious thus to skim!' I cried,
> 'By Jove! I too will try-cycle;
> And when like him I've learnt to ride,
> Why, then, I'll also buy-cycle.'
>
> That very day I made a start,
> First practising the tricycle,
> Then soaring to that nobler art,
> The riding of the bicycle.
>
> So well I liked my hired machine,
> That, having ask'd the price-ical,
> I bought it, and it since has been
> My own peculiar bicycle.
>
> And now, at morn, and noon, and night,
> My life is paradisical;
> I emulate the eagle's flight,
> When mounted on my bicycle.
>
> Oh, all ye gay and festive youth,
> Remember my advic-ical,
> And haste to prove this precious truth –
> There's nothing like the bicycle!

Walter Parke, Songs of Singularity, 1874

The King of the Road

We're all doing it now. It's glorious; the nearest approach to wings permitted to men and women here below. Intoxicating! ... And it's transforming clothes. Short jackets and cloth caps are coming in. Bustles are no more. And, my dear – *bloomers* are seen in the land! ... We're all getting most thrillingly *fin-de-siècle!*

Rose Macaulay, *Told by an Idiot*, 1923

THE BLOOMER GIRL

The arrival of the 'safety' bicycle in 1885 and the pneumatic tyre patented in 1888 made bicycling available to everyone.

One day at lunch my father said he had just seen a new kind of tyre, filled up with air, and he thought it might be a success. And soon after that everyone had bicycles, ladies and all, and bicycling became the smart thing in Society, and the lords and ladies had their pictures in the papers, riding along in the park, in straw boater hats. We were then promoted to wearing baggy knickerbockers under our frocks, and over our white frilly drawers. We thought this horridly improper, but rather grand, and when a lady (whom I didn't like anyhow) asked me, privately, to lift up my frock so that she might see the strange garments underneath, I thought what a dirty mind she had. I only saw once a woman (not of course a *lady*) in real bloomers.

Gwen Raverat, *Period Piece*, 1952

Should a 'lady' ride a bicycle at all? This was one of the questions of the day. Old traditions died hard.

If a man saw or heard of a woman riding he was horrified. 'Unwomanly. Most unwomanly! God knows what the world's coming to', but the women ... suspended judgement. They saw possibilities which they were soon to seize. ... One woman after another appeared riding a glittering new bicycle. In long skirts, it is true, but with most of their petticoats left in the bedroom behind them. ... And oh! the joy of the new means of progression, to cleave the air as though on wings, defying time and space.

Flora Thompson, *Candleford Green,* 1943

It needed women of spirit to brave the obstacles. One pioneer was the writer Edith Nesbit. Another was Ethel Smythe, who discovered the bicycle in the spring of 1890:

In the *Illustrated London News* were to be seen pictures of wild women of the usual unprepossessing pioneer type riding about Epping Forest, and I at once decided to buy a bicycle. Aunts, cousins and friends were horrified ... never has the word 'indelicate' been bandied about with more righteous conviction. Buy one I did, with bad paces too, for pneumatic tyres were not yet invented. I also took lessons at a place called Cycledom, and the scene of my first unaided attempts was, O Wonder! the gravel sweep in front of Lambeth Palace, where I even had the honour of giving instruction to the Dean of Windsor ... though for many a long day to come no 'nice' women rode bicycles. I pursued my solitary course with enthusiasm. By degrees the thing caught on, and one day, about eighteen months later when I met the arch-prude of the neighbourhood wobbling along the high road and beheld her fall off her machine at my feet to explain that she had taken to it in order to avoid having out the horses on

Sunday, it was clear that the indelicacy ghost had been finally laid.

Ethel Smythe, *Impressions that Remained,* 1923

Ladies began to pay calls on bicycles. Ethel Smythe used to cycle to friends and change into evening dress behind a bush in the garden. Changing could cause problems.

One summer evening my parents rode ten miles to dinner at Six Mile Bottom; their evening clothes were carried in cases on the handlebars. . . . But when my mother came to dress that evening she found that, though the bodice and train were there, the skirt had been left behind. . . . So she had to borrow a very inharmonious skirt from her hostess, who was much shorter and stouter than herself.

Gwen Raverat, *Period Piece,* 1952

What was a suitable cycling costume for women? There were those who argued for a radical change in women's dress. One solution was to give up long skirts altogether and take up Rational Dress. Bloomers, originating in America, became the vogue.

> Some observing man discovered
> (How I've never thought to ask)
> That Kentucky maidens' bloomers
> Have a pocket for a flask;
> That the cycling girl of Texas
> As she rides is not afraid,
> She provides a pistol pocket
> When she has her bloomers made;
> That the bloomer-girl of Boston
> Always cool and wisely frowning,
> Has a pocket in her bloomers
> Where she carries Robert Browning;
> That the Daisy Bell of Kansas,
> Who has donned the cycling breeches,

THE BLOOMER GIRL

Has a pocket in her bloomers
Full of women suffrage speeches;
That Chicago's wheeling woman
When her cycle makes rotations
Has a special bloomer pocket
Where she carries pork quotations.

Toledo *Bee*

Yes, 'Knickers' are the proper dress
Wherewith a Cycle's seat to press;
Convenient, and – should you be thrown –
Making less re-ve-la-ti-on;
There's less of danger, aye, and dirt,
Attending the divided skirt.
I will not say I wholly *like*
To see my JULIA on a 'bike';
I will not say that I should *choose*
To see Corinna don the trews;
But yet, if either beauty feel
That she is bound to cycle wheel,
(Like to a she-Ixion) then,
Since ladies aim to ride like men,
'Tis clear that all experience teaches
That it is best to wear knee-breeches,
And drop the prejudice that doth dote
On the tempestuous petticoat.
A skirt that catcheth here and there
And leaves a stretch of stocking bare,
Raiments that ruck, and cause thereby
The wheels to move confusedly;
All these be awkward follies, sure,
Compared with dual garmenture.
Knickers and leggings, by and by,
With their unfeigned simplicity,
Will more bewitch us – on a 'bike' –
Than flowing skirts we now do like!

Punch, 29 September 1894

Punch *made the most of the 'bloomer girl'.*

Fair Cyclist (wearing rational dress): Is this the way to Wareham, please?
Native: Yes, miss, yew seem to me to ha' got 'em on all right!

Punch, 6 September 1899

Niece (discussing bicycle attire): Are you as much against 'Bloomers' as ever, Uncle?
General McCurry: Certainly, my dear. It must be skirts or nothing. That is–I mean–er–
Mrs McCurry: General !!!

Punch, 19 April 1899

Most women kept to conventional dress – but they liked to look smart.

History has not recorded which of the fashionable women was first to discover the delight of whirling all over the country on two wheels; but it was certainly Lady Norreys who first excelled in this direction and I can well remember seeing quite a little crowd collected at her door in Great Cumberland Place to see her start upon her ride, when, regardless of her admiring audience, she jumped lightly on to her machine, and ringing her bell smartly once or twice as warning, wheeled away, with her dogs frisking and barking behind her. She knows nothing whatever of fear; and with quite unruffled countenance will cross that dangerous wide space between Constitution Hill and Piccadilly.... She is always very neatly dressed, generally in dark blue, with white revers on her coat and a natty sailor hat.

Mrs F. Harcourt Williamson, *The Complete Cyclist*, 1897

Women on bicycles were often considered 'unladylike'.

I remember riding with my aunt Isabel through Staines and hearing a brawny-armed woman with her sleeves rolled up say to another as my aunt rode by: 'They don't half mind showing their limbs on those machines, do they?' I suppose my aunt's ankles were just visible.

Compton MacKenzie, *My Life and Times*, 1963

But most people applauded the 'new woman'.

Go, lilt your lays to bygone days,
    When crinolines were sported;
When pretty girls wore corkscrew curls
    And beaux in stocks escorted.
Let fogies frown, and Grundys drown
    The world with wails impassioned:
What 'though they scream? I sing my theme –
    The girl who is new-fashioned.

[23]

The girl of old was good as gold,
    And with her lot contented;
Why praise her more? She lived before
    The cycle was invented.
I sing the maid in skirts arrayed
    With hint of ankles peeping,
Who mounts her wheel, and joys to feel
    Her metal steed go leaping.

No Dresden doll who loves to loll
    In Oriental languor,
In cushioned tomb, whose painted bloom
    Shrinks from the four winds' anger.
But just a girl – an English girl –
    Prepared for any juncture;
What heart could pass by such a lass
    And not receive a puncture?

> J. M. Flagg, 'The Cycling Girl'
> from *Yankee Girl Abroad*, 1900

Dress was one subject of controversy. Health was another.

In young girls the bones of the pelvis are not able to resist the tension required to ride a bicycle, and so may become more or less distorted in shape, with perhaps in after life, resulting distress.

> *Northern Wheeler*, 17 August 1892

And there were some who were alarmed for their safety.

... parents and guardians will probably only become wise after the event. Given a lonely road, and a tramp desperate with hunger or naturally vicious, and it stands to reason that a girl, or indeed any woman, riding alone must be in some considerable peril.

> Mrs F. Harcourt Williamson, *The Complete Cyclist*, 1897

The bicycle could upset the domestic apple-cart.

'Since the mistress took to riding, the staff of servants has been reduced,' deplored an under-gardener. 'You see, there are four young ladies, and they are all devotees of the wheel. The young men of the family are ardent cyclists, some of the horses have been sold, the grooms have been dismissed, and the world of the stables has fallen to the coachmen and a stable-boy. So frequently do the girls go away that it has been deemed advisable to dispense with the services of a housemaid, the cook bemoaning the loss, as many extra duties fall to her lot in consequence.'

The Hub, June 1897

The knell of the selfish, much-waited upon, old-fashioned father of the family was sounded by the bicycle bell.

Mother's out upon her bike, enjoying of the fun,
Sister and her beau have gone to take a little run.
The housemaid and the cook are both a-riding on
    their wheels;
And Daddy's in the kitchen a-cooking of the meals.

Flora Thompson, *Candleford Green*, 1943

Even a counter-attack could fail.

Henpeck'd he was. He learnt to bike.
'Now I can go just where I like',
He chuckled to himself. But she
had learnt to bike as well as he,
And, what was more, had bought a new
Machine to sweetly carry two.
Ever together now they go,
He sighing, 'this is wheel *and* woe.'

'The Biker Biked', *Mr Punch Awheel*, n.d.

WOOING THE BICYCLE

Learning to ride created its own problems. It sounded easy enough.

> To mount the wheel with perfect grace
> First see the pedals are in place;
> The right, the centre half around,
> The left, the nearest to the ground
> Draw back the wheel a little thus,
> To give it proper impetus.
> Your hands upon the handlebar
> Should be as saintly touches are,
> Then press the right foot, till you see
> The inside pedal rising free.
> Don't be in haste, the pedal right
> Describes the circle, sinks from sight;
> But ere it meets your foot, once more
> You've mounted and the lesson's o'er.
>
> Grace Duff Boylan, 1896

There were many ways of learning to ride.

When the gas-lamps are lighted, when twilight grows
     grey,
And our road is as bare as the lonely sea-shore,
I slip like a felon who's off with his prey
From the sheltering shade of our little back door.
There's a rattle of steel on the scullery floor,
Then a rustle of petticoats sweeps by my side:
In the dead of the dark we set out to explore,
For my Lady Godiva is learning to ride.

She chooses the darkness: she shrinks from the day:
She is shy of the milkman she dare not ignore:
She declares Mrs Bangs, who lives over the way,
Will watch from her window from midday till four.

[26]

So every night, when I'm weary and sore,
She leans on my shoulder with womanly pride,
And I trot by the wheel of the wife I adore;
For my Lady Godiva is learning to ride.

> 'The Ballad of the Devout Husband', from
> Arthur Waugh, *Legends of the Wheel*, n.d.

I found a whole philosophy of life in the wooing and
the winning of my bicycle . . . learning to mount: that
is the *pons asinorum* of the whole mathematical under-
taking. You have to balance your system more carefully
than you ever did your accounts: not the smallest
fraction can be out of the way, or away you go, the
treacherous steed forming one half of an equation and
yourself with a bruised knee forming the other. You
must add a stroke at just the right angle to mount,
subtract one to descend, divide them equally to hold
your seat, and multiply all these movements in definite
ratio and true proportion by the swiftest of all roots, or
you will become the most minus of quantities.

> Francis E. Willard, *A Wheel Within a Wheel*, 1895

Every woman in London apparently is learning to ride
the bicycle. The streets and parks echo to the cries of
'I'm going. I'm going, hold me back!' – 'You're all
right, I've got you' – 'Oh, don't leave me, I can't' –
'Yes, you can, mind the kerb. Don't look at your feet,
you can't fall!' – 'Oh dear, what's happened?' – 'It's all
right' – 'There you are. I knew it!' – 'Oh, that's
nothing, you'll get used to that. Jump up.'

I gather that, taking the average, a person can learn
the bicycle in six months, provided they don't miss a
single day. The lessons last about half an hour, and the
charge is from half a crown to five shillings.

> Jerome K. Jerome, *Humours of Cycling*, 1897

'It was awful. I was most fearfully rude. I shouted
'Get out of the way' and I was on the wrong side of the

road; but miles off, only I *knew* I couldn't get back. I had forgotten how to steer.'

'Hadn't you a bell?'

'Yes, but it meant sliding my hand along. I daren't do that . . . I *had* to go on, because I couldn't get off. I can wobble along, but I can't mount or dismount. I was never so frightened in my life.' . . . 'You've really had a lesson. . . . Tell us all about it. Have you been out alone yet?'

They leaned across the table and spoke low, one after the other. 'We went out – last night – after dark – and rode – round Russell Square – twice – in our knickers.'

'No! Did you really? How simply heavenly.'

'It *was*. We came home nearly crying with rage at not being able to go about, permanently, in nothing but knickers. It would make life an *absolutely* different thing.'

'The freedom of movement.'

'Exactly. You feel like a sprite you are so light.'

'And like a poet though you don't know it . . .'

'Yes, and it is not only that; think of never having to brush your skirt.'

'Then you can both really ride?'

'We do nothing else; we've given up walking: we no longer walk up and down stairs; we ride.'

Dorothy Richardson, *Pilgrimage*, 1919

A girl, a wheel,
A shock, a squeal,
A header, a thump,
A girl in a lump,
A bloomer all torn,
A maiden forlorn.

Wrecked, Anon.

In London the fashionable place to learn and to ride was Battersea Park.

In Battersea Park, any morning between eleven and one, all the best blood in England could be seen, solemnly pedalling up and down the half-mile drive that runs between the river and the refreshment kiosk. ... In shady by-paths elderly countesses, perspiring peers, still in the wobbly stage, battled bravely with the laws of equilibrium; occasionally defeated, would fling their arms round the necks of hefty young hooligans who were reaping a rich harvest as cycling instructors: proficiency guaranteed in twelve lessons.

Jerome K. Jerome, *My Life and Times,* 1926

Some learned to ride in quieter spots.

In the Easter of 1895 Mrs Webb made up a party for a week's stay at the little hotel which stands at the top of Beachy Head. Besides themselves and myself, Shaw, Wallas and Charles Trevelyan were there. In the intervals between unending talks about things in general, we seized the opportunity to learn, on the short quiet stretch of level road along the top of the cliff, how to ride the 'safety' bicycle, that was then just coming into vogue. Wallas and Trevelyan, who had already acquired the art, were instructors to the rest of us.

Viscount Samuel, *Memoirs*, 1945

Mrs Webb seems to have got the hang of it.

I have a little picture in my mind of Mrs Webb, who rode extremely well, scudding on before us down one of the back streets of Pimlico . . . with both hands behind her back, steering by her pedals. She was a graceful and intrepid rider, and indeed we all fancied ourselves very much on our machines.

Amy Strachey, *St. Loe Strachey, his Life and his Paper*, 1930

Others, however, never acquired the knack – but you could at least hope for a helping hand.

Mother walked the four miles to the shops. . . . When she tired of this, she'd borrow Dorothy's bicycle, though she never quite mastered the machine. Happy enough when the thing was in motion, it was stopping and starting that puzzled her. She had to be launched on her way by running parties of villagers; and to stop she rode into a hedge. With the Stroud Co-op Stores, where she was a registered customer, she had come to a special arrangement. This depended for its success upon a quick ear and timing, and was a beautiful operation to watch. As she coasted downhill towards the shop's main entrance, she would let out one of her screams; an assistant, specially briefed, would tear through the shop, out the side door, and catch her in his arms. He had to be both young and nimble, for if he missed her she piled up by the police-station.

Laurie Lee, *Cider With Rosie*, 1959

It was not only women who had difficulty in learning to ride. H. G. Wells described how Mr Hoopdriver, the first cycling hero in fiction, coped with the task.

There is only one phrase to describe his course at this stage, and that is – voluptuous curves. He did not ride fast, he did not ride straight, an exacting critic might say he did not ride well   but he rode generously, opulently, using the whole road and even nibbling at the footpath. The excitement never flagged. So far he had never passed or been passed by anything, but as yet the day was young, and the road was clear. He doubted his steering so much that, for the present, he had resolved to dismount at the approach of anything else upon wheels. The shadows of the trees lay very long and blue across the road; the morning sunlight was like amber fire. ... Whoops for Freedom and Adventure. . . . Talk of your *joie de vivre!*

H. G. Wells, *The Wheels of Chance,* 1896

It was easy to be romantic about cycling – but the rhythm could be nightmarish.

After your first day of cycling one dream is inevitable. A memory of motion lingers in the muscles of your legs, and round and round they seem to go. You ride through dreamland on wonderful dream bicycles that change and grow; you ride down steeples and stair-cases and over precipices; you hover in horrible suspense over inhabited towns, vainly seeking for a brake your hand cannot find, to save you from a head-long fall; you plunge into weltering rivers and rush helplessly at monstrous obstacles. ... Where the devil was the brake? It must have fallen off. And the bell? Right in front of him was Guildford. He tried to shout and warn the town to get out of the way but his voice was gone as well. Nearer, nearer! it was fearful! and in another moment the houses were cracking like nuts, and the blood of the inhabitants squirting this way and that. The streets were black with people running. . . . A feeling of horror came upon Mr Hoopdriver: he flung himself sideways to descend, forgetting how high he was and forthwith he began falling, falling, falling.

ibid.

Well, you're driving like mad with this singular lad
    (by the by, the ship's now a four-wheeler),
And you're playing round games, and he calls you bad
    names when you tell him that 'ties pay the dealer';
But this you can't stand, so you throw up your hand,
    and you find you're as cold as an icicle,
In your shirt and your socks (the black silk with gold
    clocks), crossing Salisbury Plain on a bicycle . . .

From W. S. Gilbert, *Iolanthe*

COME RIDE WITH ME

The great year for cycling was 1895:

The year I mean is the one in whose spring-time we all went bicycling (O thrill!) in Battersea Park, and ladies wore sleeves that billowed enormously out from their shoulders and Lord Rosebery was Prime Minister.

Max Beerbohm, *Seven Men and Two Others*, 1950

Everyone was riding, everyone was talking about it: it brought a sense of freedom and exhilaration.

It alters everything. To be able to bicycle would make life utterly different; on a bicycle you feel a different person; nothing can come near you, you forget who you are. Aren't you glad you are alive today when all these things are happening?

Dorothy Richardson, *Pilgrimage*, 1919

Partaker in my happiest mood,
Companion of my solitude
Refuge when gloomy thoughts intrude,
My bicycle to you I sing!
With you no cares my brain oppress,
I laugh at fortune's fickleness;
No other sports your charm possess,
Nor match for me the joy you bring.

The Cycling Magazine, October 1896

Stanley pedalled swiftly, a sturdy attractive figure in serge knickerbockers . . . along a smooth, sandy road between pine woods. The April sunlight flickered on the pale, brown, needle-strewn road: the light wind sang in the pines and blew dark curls of hair from under Stanley's sailor hat-brim. Her bicycle basket was full of primroses. Her round, brown cheeks glowed pink: her lips were parted in a low, tuneless song. . . . It expressed her happiness, relieved the pressure of her joy at being alive. Such a day! Such a bicycle! Such sweet and merry air! . . . Before her there was a long slope down. To take it, brakeless, feet up on the rest, was like flying.

Rose Macaulay, *Told By an Idiot*, 1928

The Glory of the Holidays had resumed its sway with a sudden accession of splendour. At the crest of the hill he put his feet upon the foot rests, and now, riding moderately straight, went, with a palpitating brake, down that excellent descent. A new delight was in his eyes, quite over and above the pleasure of rushing through the keen, sweet morning air. He reached out his thumb and twanged his bell out of sheer happiness.

H. G. Wells, *Wheels of Chance*, 1896

With lifted feet, hands still,
I am poised, and down the hill
Dart, with heedful mind;
The air goes by in a wind.

Swifter and yet more swift,
Till the heart with a mighty lift
Makes the lungs laugh, the throat cry:—
'O bird, see; see, bird, I fly!

'Is this, is this your joy?
O bird, then I, though a boy,
For a golden moment share
Your feathery life in air!'

Say, heart, is there aught like this
In a world that is full of bliss?
'Tis more than skating, bound
Steel-shod to the level ground.

Speed slackens now, I float
Awhile in my airy boat;
Till, when the wheels scarce crawl,
My feet to the treadles fall.

Alas, that the longest hill
Must end in a vale; but still,
Who climbs with toil, whereso'er,
Shall find wings waiting there.

Henry Charles Beeching,
Going Down Hill on a Bicycle

Lifted off the earth, sitting at rest in the moving air, the London air turning into fresh moving air flowing through your head, the green squares and high houses moving, sheering smoothly along, sailing towards you changed, upright and alive, moving by, speaking, telescoping away, behind unforgotten, still visible, staying in your forward-looking eyes, being added to in unbroken movement, a whole, moving silently to the sound of firm white tyres circling on smooth wood, echoing through the endless future to the riding ring of the little bell, ground easily out by firm new cogs. . . . Country roads flowing by in sun and shadow; the ring of the bell making the hedges brilliant at empty turnings . . . all there in your mind with dew and freshness as you threaded round and round and in and out of the maze of squares in evening light; consuming the evening time by leaving you careless and strong.

Dorothy Richardson, *Pilgrimage*, 1919

Cycling was fun and it inspired a wealth of doggerel, often in the style of a well-known poet. G. K. Chesterton could well have inspired this poem by a veteran of the Boston Bicycle Club, the first cycling club in America.

We're the healthy, happy heathen, the Men Who Ride
 for Fun,
The faithful friends of bicycling, that sport surpassed
 by none.
We've ridden through long seasons past; we'll ride
 long seasons more;
And while we've gained both health and strength, we
 have had fun galore.

We're close to Mother Nature, and she greets us every
 year
With blossoming flowers, budding trees and sunny
 atmosphere.
We hear her voice low-calling, just as soon as spring's
 begun.
She tells her choicest secrets to the Men Who Ride
 for Fun.

We start the season's wheeling when the frost first
 leaves the ground.
We know the roads in every town for fifty miles around.

Our minds are clear, our hearts are light, digestion
    Number One.
We've three big appetites a day, the Men Who Ride
    for Fun.

There are men who ride for exercise and men who ride
    for health.
There are men who ride for mileage and men who ride
    for speed,
And once men rode for fashion, but they quickly
    petered out,
And are giving their attention now to nervousness
    and gout.

There are men who ride for mileage and men who
    ride for speed,
And in a few short seasons they get all the wheel they
    need
While we keep on year after year; our wheeling's
    never done.
We hearty, hungry vagabonds, the Men Who Ride
    for Fun.

We wear each other's burdens and enjoy each other's
    jokes;
Respect each other's feelings and the rights of other
    folks.
Bring out your wheels and join us. You'll be welcome,
    everyone,
To the Brothers of the Bicycle, the Men Who Ride
    for Fun.

Dr Walter G. Kendall, *The Men Who Ride for Fun*

*Riding fast was the great thrill. Scorchers, as they were
called, became a menace and provoked angry letters in*
The Times.

I know I'm a 'scorcher', I know I am torcher
　To buffers and mivvies who're not up to date;
But grumpy old geesers, and wobbly old wheezers,
　Ain't goin' to wipe me and my wheel orf the slate.
I mean to go spinning and 'owling and grinning
　At twelve mile an hour through the thick of the throng.
And shout, without stopping, whilst, frightened and
　　flopping,
　My elderly victims like ninepins are dropping, –
'So long!'

From 'Song of the Scorcher', Mr Punch Awheel

*For a decade the bicycle was the king of the road. Every-
one was riding and everyone flocked to the countryside.*

A bike, a bike! My kingdom for a bike!
And when the price is normal I will tell you what
　　I'd like:
A ride through corn-lands redly ripe, or 'meads with
　　daisies pied';
With comfort in my haversack and beauty by my side.
Through dewy morn, through noonday glow, through
　　twilight's tender grey,
Along the dales and over the hills,
　And far away!

Robert Blatchford, As I Lay Thinking, n.d.

After midnight on the morning of 21 June 1908 I set
off for Stonehenge. . . . After the cock ceased crowing a
tawny owl began to hoot, and the long, tremulous
mellow sound followed me for some distance from the
village and then there was perfect silence, broken
occasionally by the tinkling bells of a little company of
cyclists speeding past towards 'The Stones'. . . . At
Stonehenge I found a good number of watchers, about
a couple of hundred already assembled, but more were
coming in continually and a mile or so of the road to
Amesbury visible from 'The Stones' had at times the

appearance of a ribbon of fire from the lamps of this continuous stream of coming cyclists. Altogether about five or six hundred persons gathered at 'The Stones' mostly young men on bicycles who came from all the Wiltshire towns within easy distance, from Salisbury to Bath.

W. H. Hudson, *Afoot in England*, 1909

It's ho! for a ride in the open,
  With the cool winds blowing free,
And nothing but joy on dale and hill
  For my trusty wheel and me,
It's ho! for the dew of the morning
  That sparkles on leaf and spray,
And ho! for the charm of the sunset light
  When the glad day fades away.
With muscles that answer quickly
  To call of the resolute will,
With cheeks that glow and eyes that shine
  And pulses that bound and thrill,
I fly through the beautiful kingdom
  That beckons my wheel and me,
Queen of the world of girlhood,
  And sovereign of all I see.

Margaret E. Sangster, *Ho! For the Wheel*

A favourite haunt for cyclists was the London to Portsmouth Road near Hindhead.

The run from Hindhead down to Godalming will remain long in memory. The road was perfect; it was about mid-day, and exceedingly hot; but the rapid motion made a breeze, which seemed to insulate me from the flames. There was no one else on the road for the seven miles of descent; and this was perhaps as well, for my spirits were so much raised that I could not help shouting. I thought of Elijah going to heaven in a chariot of fire, and extinguished a scruple about the

downward direction by a vague reference to Antipodes.
Every now and then the wind brought a hot whiff of the
bramble, and the aromatic smell of firs ... I was so
much cheered by the journey that I conceived a tenderness for any bicyclists I met, and would have accosted
them had they not looked strangely on me. There
should be (perhaps there is) some formal salutation for
the road, or better several, one for meeting on a level,
one for encouragement to the bicyclist going up hill,
one for congratulation to the fortunate brother going
down.

Henry Charles Beeching, *Pages from a Private Diary*, 1899

*For some cycling was not just a pleasure. It became a
passion – and the bicycle itself an object of worship.*

How my father did adore those bicycles! Such beautiful machines. They were as carefully tended as if they
had been alive; every speck of dust or wet was wiped
from them as soon as we came back from a ride; and at
night they were all brought into the house, and slung
up to the ceiling of the kitchen passage by a series of
ingenious pulleys, for fear that the night air in the
covered backyard might rust them.

Gwen Raverat, *Period Piece*, 1952

I went out to the back garden ... and found Father
and Jack ... busy on an upturned bicycle, the pride of
Father's heart. With greasy rags and an odd-shaped
brush, they were polishing the gun-metal hubs and
the rims of the wheels, selecting each spoke for separate
attention, so that the little nuts and nipples joining the
spokes to the rims shone like jewels.

Richard Church, *Over the Bridge*, 1955

There are two ways you can get exercise out of a
bicycle. You can 'overhaul' it, or you can ride it. On
the whole I am not sure that a man who takes his

pleasure overhauling does not have the best of the bargain. He is independent of the weather and the wind; the state of the road troubles him not. Give him a screw-hammer, a bundle of rags, an oil can and something to sit down upon, and he is happy for the day. He has to put up with certain disadvantages, of course, there is no joy without alloy. He himself always looks like a tinker, and his machine always suggests the idea that, having stolen it, he has tried to disguise it; but as he rarely gets beyond the first mile-stone with it, this, perhaps, does not much matter. The mistake some people make is in thinking they can get both forms of sport out of the same machine. This is impossible; no machine will stand the double strain.

Jerome K. Jerome, *Three Men on the Bummel*, 1900

The romance of cycling was greatly fostered by advertising.

On only one poster that I can recollect have I seen the rider represented as doing any work. But then this man was being pursued by a bull. In ordinary cases the object of the artist is to convince the hesitating neophyte that the sport of bicycling consists in sitting on a luxurious saddle, and being moved rapidly in the direction you wish to go by unseen heavenly powers.

Generally speaking, the rider is a lady, and then one feels that, for perfect bodily rest combined with entire freedom from mental anxiety, slumber upon a water-bed cannot compare with bicycle riding upon a hilly road. No fairy travelling on a summer cloud could take things more easily than does the bicycle girl, according to the poster. . . . Less often it is a mere male thing that rides the machine. He is not so accomplished an acrobat as is the lady; but simple tricks, such as standing on the saddle and waving flags, drinking beer or beef-tea while riding, he can and does perform. . . . And the sun is always shining, and the roads are always dry. No stern parent rides behind, no interfering aunt beside, no demon small boy brother is peeping round the corner, there never comes a skid.

ibid.

The reality was, of course, different. One was likely to have, as Mr Polly put it, 'little accidentulous misadventures'.

'Stout elderly gentleman – shirt sleeves – large straw wastepaper basket sort of hat – starts to cross the road – going to the oil shop – prodic refreshment of oil can –'

'Don't say you run 'im down,' said Mrs Larkins, gasping. 'Don't say you run 'im down, Elfrid!'

'Run 'im down! Not me, Madam; I never run anything down. Wabble. Ring the bell. Wabble, wabble –'

'No one's going to run him down. Hears the bell! Wabble. Gust of wind. Off comes the hat smack into the wheel. Wabble. *Lord! what's* going to happen? Hat across the road, old gentleman after it, bell, shriek. He ran into me. Didn't ring his bell, hadn't *got* a bell – just ran into me. Over I went clinging to his venerable head. Down he went with me clinging to him. Oil can blump, blump into the road. . . . But that's the sort of thing that is constantly happening, you know – on a bicycle. People run into you, hens, and cats, and dogs, and things. Everything seems to have its mark on you; everything.

H. G. Wells, *The History of Mr Polly*, 1910

But these were not the only hazards.

As I started now to pedal out into the great world, I was icily sober, and the old skill, in consequence, had deserted me entirely. I found myself wobbling badly, and all the stories I had ever heard of nasty bicycle accidents came back to me with a rush . . . my thoughts [were] diverted by the sudden necessity of zigzagging sharply in order to avoid a pig in the fairway . . . but fortunately a quick zig on my part, coinciding with an adroit zag on the part of the pig, enabled me to win through, and I continued my ride safe, but with the heart fluttering like a captive bird.

The effect of this narrow squeak upon me was to shake the nerve to the utmost. The fact that pigs were abroad in the night seemed to bring home to me the perilous nature of my enterprise. It set me thinking of all the other things that could happen to a man out and about on a velocipede without a lamp after lighting-up time. In particular, I recalled the statement of a pal of mine that in certain sections of the rural districts goats were accustomed to stray across the road to the extent of their chains, thereby forming about as sound a booby trap as one could well wish. . . . And there was one chap who ran into an elephant, left over from a travelling circus.

P. G. Wodehouse, *Carry on, Jeeves*, 1925

Pigs, goats, elephants – they were not the only creatures to have a hard time of it.

Two or three seasons ago I was so unfortunate as to run over a large and beautifully bright grass snake near Aldermaston, once a snake sanctuary. He writhed and wriggled in the road as if I had broken his back, but on picking him up I was pleased to find that my wind-inflated rubber tyre had not, like the brazen chariot wheel, crushed his delicate vertebrae; he quickly recovered and when released glided swiftly and easily away into cover. Twice only have I deliberately tried to run down, to tread on coat-tails, so to speak, of any wild creature. One was a weasel, the other a stoat, running along at a hedge-side before me. In both instances, just as the front wheel was touching the tail, the little flat-headed rascal swerved quickly aside and escaped.

W. H. Hudson, *Afoot in England,* 1924

After the turn of the century there was a new threat to the cyclist – the motor car.

His bicycle was now very old, and it is one of the concomitants of a bicycle's senility that its free-wheel should one day obstinately cease to be free. It corres-ponds to that epoch in human decay when an old gentleman loses his incisor teeth. It happened just as Mr Polly was approaching Mr Rusper's shop, and the untoward chance of a motor car trying to pass a wagon on the wrong side gave Mr Polly no choice but to get on to the pavement and dismount. ... Mr Polly found himself among the various sonorous things with which Mr Rusper adorned the front of his shop – zinc dust bins, household pails, lawn mowers, rakes, spades, and all manner of clattering things. ... He sent a column of pails thundering across the doorway, and dismounted with one foot in a sanitary dustbin, amidst an enormous uproar of falling ironmongery. ... Mr Rusper laid one hand on the bicycle handle, and the other gripped Mr Polly's collar urgently. Whereupon Mr Polly said 'Leggo!' and again 'D'you *hear*? Leggo!' and then drove his elbow with considerable force into the region of Mr Rusper's midriff. Whereupon Mr Rusper, with a loud impassioned cry resembling 'Woo kik' more than any other combination of letters, released the bicycle handle, seized Mr Polly by the cap and hair, and bore his head and shoulders downwards. Thereat Mr Polly ... butted his utmost into the concavity of Mr Rusper, entwined a leg about him, and, after terrific moments of swaying instability, fell headlong beneath him amidst the bicycle and pails.

H. G. Wells, *The History of Mr Polly*, 1910

For a few years one new mechanical marvel ran neck and neck with the other. On 31 January 1900 The Irish Cyclist reported that the Chief Constable of Surrey had bought 125 Singer bicycles to set up a special squad of policemen to overtake and halt motorists who exceeded the speed limit of 12 miles per hour. Conan Doyle, too, was quick to see the opportunities the bicycle afforded for crime and detection.

We had come on a small black ribbon of pathway. In the middle of it, clearly marked on the sodden soil, was the track of a bicycle.

'A bicycle certainly, but not *the* bicycle', said Holmes. 'I am familiar with forty-two different impressions left by tyres. This, as you perceive is a Dunlop, with a patch upon the outer cover. Heidegger's tyres were Palmers, leaving longitudinal stripes. ... The more deeply sunk impression is, of course, the hind wheel, upon which the weight rests. You

perceive several places where it has passed across and
obliterated the more shallow mark of the front one.
It was undoubtedly heading away from the school. . . .
Do you observe that the rider is now undoubtedly
forcing the pace? Look at this impression, where you
get both tyres clear. The one is as deep as the other.
That can only mean that the rider is throwing his
weight on to the handle-bar as a man does when he is
sprinting. By Jove, he has had a fall.' There was a
broad irregular smudge covering some yards of the
track. Then there were a few footmarks, and the tyre
reappeared once more.

'A side slip', I suggested. . . . The tracks of the tyre
began to curve fantastically upon the wet and shining
path. Suddenly, as I looked ahead, the gleam of metal
caught my eye from amid the thick gorse bushes. Out
of them we dragged a bicycle, Palmer-tyred, one pedal
bent, and the whole front of it horribly smeared and
slobbered with blood.

Sir Arthur Conan Doyle,
The Adventure of the Priory School, 1904

*But before long the cyclist had clearly lost his place as
King of the Road and had been pushed to the dusty verge.
Some even gave up the bicycle altogether.*

Of all the vile inventions misbegotten by mistake
The thing they call the bicycle does surely take the cake,
'E's ugly an 'e's vulgar, and 'e's dangerous to ride,
An' he fills the man as rides 'im with a sort of beastly
    pride.

Oh, the bike, oh the bike! oh, the scarin', tarin' Bike!
'E's just a 'oly terror going scorchin' down the road
With a grinnin' idiot clingin' to the 'andles monkey-
    like
'is shoulders 'unched above 'im like a 'umpy sort o toad.

You think you'll learn to ride 'im coz it don't look
    'ard at all
But you've got to get acquainted just with every kind of
    fall,
You've got to learn 'ow gravel feels a-stickin' in your
    jaw
And what it is to have your knees and knuckles
    always raw.

Oh the bike! Oh, the bike! oh the lanky, cranky bike!
'E's twenty ways of fallin' down, an' can't stand up
    alone.
If there's a stone within a mile you can be sure 'e'll
    strike;
'E tumbles down and chucks you, and it's odds you
    breaks a bone.

'The Bicycle Craze' (with apologies to Rudyard
Kipling), from *Humours of Cycling*

DAISY RINGS A BELL

*A popular variant of the bicycle was the tandem. There
was something particularly romantic about it.*

The pedals flew, the rubber rim
Spun round and on. The very brim
Of summer's joy flowed full and sweet
For two young hearts that throbbing beat
And Cupid's fluttering wings were spread
Where swift their tandem sprang and sped.
With quickening breath and shining eyes
He saw the glowing colour rise
In waves upon her rounded cheek.
He bent his head close down to speak
Four words that only lovers know,
He whispered low – 'I love you so.'

Outing, 1898

Their engagement ran through a halcyon summer. . . .
They bought a tandem bicycle and pedalled all over
Long Island – which Mrs Cassius Ruthven, a con-
temporary Cato, considered 'rather fast' for a couple
not yet married.

F. Scott Fitzgerald, *What a Handsome Pair*, 1932

There is a flower within my heart,
Daisy Daisy!
Planted one day by a glancing dart,
Planted by Daisy Bell!
Whether she loves me or loves me not,
Sometimes it's hard to tell;
Yet I am longing to share the lot
Of beautiful Daisy Bell!
   (*Refrain*) Daisy, Daisy, Give me your answer do!
   I'm half crazy all for the love of you!
   It won't be a stylish marriage,
   I can't afford a carriage,
   But you'll look sweet on the seat
   Of a bicycle built for two!

We will go 'tandem' as man and wife,
Daisy Daisy!
Ped'ling a-way down the road of life,
I and my Daisy Bell!
When the road's dark we can both despise
P'licemen and 'lamps' as well;
There are 'bright lights' in the dazzling eyes
Of beautiful Daisy Bell!

I will stand by you in 'wheel' or woe,
Daisy Daisy!
You'll be the bell(e) which I'll ring, you know!
Sweet little Daisy Bell!

You'll take the 'lead' in each 'trip' we take,
Then if I don't do well,
I will permit you to use the brake,
My beautiful Daisy Bell!

Harry Dacre, 1892

Yet the tandem had its own particular snags.

We had a tandem tricycle. Ken sat behind, and had the steering, the bell and the brake under his control; I sat in front and had the accident. Sharing a bed is really nothing compared with sharing a tandem tricycle. Bent double against a head-wind on a hill, the one in front feels, with every labouring breath, more and more certain that the one behind is hanging his feet over the handle-bars and looking at the scenery; and the one behind . . . is just as convinced that he is doing all the work himself and that the one in front is merely going through the motions of an entirely unfounded exhaustion.

A. A. Milne, *It's Too Late Now*, 1939

Learning to ride it wasn't easy.

'Now boys', cried Father. 'We'll have a lesson in mounting! . . .' Father brought forward the smaller tandem, as proud of it as a cavalry officer of his horse . . . I took my position beside the rear saddle of the tandem, while Jack held the front handlebars. Father seized my right foot and my posterior, hoisted me into the saddle, explaining at the same time how I must push off on the right pedal, in time with Jack. After several repetitions of this exercise, we tried the process together, and to my terror I found myself in the saddle and the tandem rushing up the yard. Jack, not used to the length and weight behind him, wobbled and applied the brake. Whereupon I fell off and barked my shin on the rat-trap pedal. But again I dared not give in, and for the rest of the afternoon we went through the movements of mounting and dismounting until by tea-time the ritual was mastered and I felt some confidence, though by now Jack was bored and grumpy. Father, however, was jubilant. He patted us on our strained and aching backs, and promised us a real ride next day.

Richard Church, *Over the Bridge,* 1955

A family tandem ride on Boxing Day went like this:

Father wore a short covert coat of fawn, a cap, knicker-bockers, stockings and spats. Mother veiled her straw hat as though she were a bee-keeper, fastened the edges of her skirt with clips and yards of elastic to the instep of her shoes, and carried a little fox-fur tippet round her neck. . . . Mother and Father mounted and left the mooring of the kerbstone. 'Come on', said Jack, 'or we shall lose sight of them.'

I shivered, gulped and obeyed. . . . We were afloat. We glided on and the pedals carried my feet round with them. . . . I could do nothing but hang on, my hands convulsive on the brown felt grips. . . . Our parents were sailing on ahead and I heard Father call aloud: 'Come along, boys, keep close.' His voice floated merrily over the ghostly parish. . . . Nothing quelled his high spirits . . . and he still had all his breath to feed that flood of conversation, buoyed up on outbursts of song . . .

'Oh merry goes the day
When the heart is young' . . .

Our tandem was built not of light alloys, but of the steel that was the chief foundation of the British Empire . . . I felt as though I were propelling the whole of the steel industry at each rise of the pedals. But Jack did not think so. He grumbled at me for being a mere passenger and he was probably right . . . I began to feel miserable, and I looked at Mother, but she was still veiled and she sat behind Father like Patience upon the monument, though I was certain she was not smiling. . . . But the veiled figure of Patience suddenly came to life, and an angry life. She insisted on dismounting. . . . She cursed the tandems, their weight, their length, their manoeuvrability. . . . She called upon God to witness the universal unfairness between the sexes, with women as the eternal victim and slave. . . . At last Mother's breath gave out. She stopped and drew me to her as though we were now to face the spears of a hostile tribe, or the rifles of a firing party.

'That's all right, old girl,' said Father. 'We'll take a short cut home over Battersea Bridge.'

ibid.

Family cycling had its problems – but there were worse disasters.

I was thinking of a tale my Uncle Cyril used to tell me as a child. An absurd little story, sir, though I confess that I have always found it droll. According to my Uncle Cyril two men named Nicholls and Jackson set out to ride to Brighton on a tandem bicycle, and were so unfortunate as to come into collision with a brewer's van. And when the rescue party arrived on the scene of the accident, it was discovered that they had been hurled together with such force that it was impossible to sort them out at all adequately. The keenest eye could not discern which portion of the fragments was Nicholls and which Jackson. So they collected as much as they could, and called it Nixon. I remember laughing very much at that story when I was a child, sir.

P. G. Wodehouse, *Carry On, Jeeves*, 1925

THE LITERARY CYCLIST

Yes; bicycling's a capital thing for a literary man.
G. B. Shaw, *Collected Letters*, 1965

Shaw was one of the early enthusiasts for the bicycle although it is hard to understand why. He was decidedly accident-prone – but game.

At Beachy Head I have been trying to learn the bicycle; and after a desperate struggle, renewed on two successive days, I will do twenty yards and a destructive fall against any professional in England. My God, the stiffness, the blisters, the bruises, the pains in every twisted muscle, the crashes against the chalk road that I have endured – and at my age too. But I shall come like gold from the furnace: I will not be beaten by that hellish machine.

Shaw to Janet Achurch, 13 April 1895. From *Collected Letters*

Later that year he was staying with Beatrice and Sidney Webb at the Argoed, their house in Wales.

The other evening, after riding over thirty miles up hill and down dale, and finishing by fifteen miles at full speed to escape being overtaken by darkness (I had left my lamp at home), I was so abominably tired after pushing the thing up the lane that when I mounted to try and ride a level bit, I tumbled off. I thought I was alighting on a grass strip by the way side; but it was a briar bush which let me gracefully down to the bottom of a deep ditch. The bicycle fell over me across the top of the ditch, and as I lay there looking up peacefully at the moon through the spokes of the wheel and the laced thorntwigs of the briar, I felt blessedly happy and at rest. It required the strongest exertion of my common sense to get up and force myself on to the house.

Shaw to Janet Achurch, 31 August 1895

A fortnight later he had a sorrier tale to tell.

On Thursday afternoon I was flying down a steep hill on the Chepstow Road, with my feet up on the rests, going at a speed that took the machine miles beyond my control. A friend of ours named Russell ... was in front of me; and Webb was behind me. Seeing the road clear before us, I gave myself up to the enjoyment of a headlong tearing toboggan down the hill. Imagine my feelings when I saw Russell jump off and turn his machine right across my path to read a signpost! ... I rang my bell and swerved desperately to the right: he looked round and backed with his machine to the right – my right – also. Then – smash. In the last second, I managed to make a twist to the left which prevented my going into him absolutely at right angles; but the catastrophe was appalling enough in all conscience as it was. Russell, fortunately, was not even scratched; but his knickerbockers were demolished – how, I don't know. ... My front wheel, which took the whole shock, behaved nobly. ... As for me, I flew through the air for several yards, and then smote the earth like a thunderbolt, literally hip and thigh – also shoulder, very hard, and wrists. 'All right' I shouted (as if there were any hurry about it now), 'I am not hurt' and bounded up, pulling myself all together instinctively. . . . I picked up my bike and trundled it up the hill. At the top, I felt sick, and the hills and clouds and farmhouses began to tumble about drunkenly. I sat down by the roadside. . . . In ten minutes I got up, mounted my staggering bike after jumping on the wheel until it became moderately round, and rode to our destination (Tintern Abbey) and back to the Argoed – about 15 or 16 miles . . . I am not thoroughly convinced yet that I was not killed. Anybody but a vegetarian would have been. Nobody but a teetotaller would have faced a bicycle again for six months.

Shaw to Janet Achurch, 16 September 1895

Bertrand Russell put a different gloss on the story.

Shaw and I were involved in a bicycle accident. . . . He was only just learning to ride a bicycle and he ran into my machine with such force that he was hurled through the air and landed on his back twenty feet from the place of collision. However he got up completely unhurt and continued his ride; whereas my bicycle was smashed, and I had to return by train. It was a very slow train and at every station Shaw with his bicycle appeared on the platform, put his head into the carriage and jeered. I suspect that he regarded the whole incident as proof of the virtues of vegetarianism.

Bertrand Russell, *Portraits from Memory*, 1956

A year later Shaw had an even more alarming accident.

One afternoon in the middle of July, I was riding in Pall Mall East when a Great Western Railway van, coming out of the Haymarket, turned up Pall Mall on its wrong side owing to the horse shying at something, and charged me point blank. It was a pretty piece of tournamenting. I went ahead gallantly, and hit the horse fair and square on the breastbone with my front tyre, fully believing that the most impetuous railway van must go down before the onslaught of Bernard Shaw. But it didn't. I hit the dust like the Templar before the lance of Ivanhoe; and though I managed to roll over and spring upright with an acrobatic bound just clear of the wheels, my bike came out a mangled, shrieking corpse. It was rather exciting for a sedentary literary man like myself.

Shaw to R. Golding Bright, 22 September 1896

Eventually he became philosophic about his accidents.

I have been taking my annual bicycle accident; and the left side of my face is temporarily obliterated. At present I look like a fearfully punished prizefighter at the end of the hundredth round.

Shaw to Graham Wallas, 16 November 1897

Shaw was not the only artist to take a tumble. For the painter Renoir a fall had more serious consequences as it was probably the beginning of the arthritis which crippled him in later years.

As Renoir was riding along on his bicycle on that rainy day in 1897 he skidded in a puddle of water and fell on a heap of stones. When he got up, he realized that he had broken his right arm. He left his bicycle in the ditch and returned home on foot, only thankful that he was ambidextrous. . . . Dr Bordes . . . put Renoir's arm in a plaster cast and advised him not to do any more bicycling. My father had therefore to paint with his left hand, and he was obliged to ask my mother to prepare his palette and to wipe off with a piece of cloth dipped in turpentine those parts of the picture that did not satisfy him. It was the first time he had ever asked anyone to help him with his work.

Jean Renoir, *Renoir, My Father*, 1962

Arnold Bennett was another to suffer at the wheel.

Bicycling is the rage now. I got my machine about 3 weeks ago ... I find cycling a most excellent practice. Weather permitting, I spend the afternoons upon two wheels, & coming home in a disgusting state of healthiness, work like Hades from 6 to 10 or thereabouts. It is noble, I tell you. Distances entirely disappear.

> Bennett to George Sturt, 31 March 1896.
> From *The Letters of Arnold Bennett,* Vol. II, 1968

A year later, however, he recorded in his Journal:

Sunday 21 March. Bicycle accident. Dislocation of the elbow. Chloroform operation 22 March. I carried my arm in splints for a month, and in a sling for six weeks. For three weeks I dictated all articles and letters. The orderliness of my existence was never so deranged before.

> *The Journals of Arnold Bennett,* 1932

But he was not deterred from cycling.

We rode out of Ipswich at dusk, with rain coming on, a high wind whistling behind us in the telegraph wires, and every sign of a stormy night. We had scarcely climbed the hill from the town when an incoming cyclist warned us of bad roads; and indeed the roads proved worse than his account of them. Nevertheless we rode every foot of the twelve miles to this place. Soon after 9.30 it was quite dark, the rain was coming down steadily, the wind (fortunately at our backs) had increased, and we were riding warily across a wild, naked country on a road of which the narrow cart-ruts formed the only rideable surface; all else was loose sand, sticky and dangerous with rain. . . .

The rain gradually penetrated our clothing and settled in our shoes, till my feet at least were stone cold.

At every few yards we started a rabbit or a stoat or some unrecognisable creature of the night. ... My lamp went out, and on dismounting I found that my invalid right arm was useless, and so we walked the last mile to a hotel in the pouring rain. .... Yet, underneath this surface discontent, discomfort and sick imagination, there was a sense of deep satisfaction, the satisfaction of facing and overcoming difficulties, of slowly achieving a desired end, in spite of obstacles.

Felixstowe, Friday 18 June 1897, ibid.

For Bennett cycling was therapeutic. After working on the last 5,000 words of Anna of the Five Towns *continuously for seventeen hours he wrote in his journal,*

I was very pleased with it; slept well for four hours, got up with a frightful headache, and cycled through Hemel Hempstead to St. Albans, lunched at the George, and home – forty-two miles.

ibid., 1902

H. G. Wells was enchanted with the bicycle.

I learnt to ride my bicycle upon sandy tracks with no one but God to help me; he chastened me considerably in the process ... the bicycle in those days was still very primitive. The diamond frame had appeared but there was no free wheel. Consequently you were often carried on beyond your intentions. ... Nevertheless the bicycle was the swiftest thing upon the roads in those days ... and the cyclist had a lordliness, a sense of masterful adventure, that has gone from him altogether now.

H. G. Wells, *Experiment in Autobiography,* 1934

The bicycle was a handy new means of running an errand of mercy. In the summer of 1898, when Wells was seriously ill, Henry James and Philip Gosse cycled over from Rye

*to see him at New Romney, and to enquire discreetly
whether he needed financial help from the Royal Literary
Fund. At the end of the following year, when the American
writer Stephen Crane was taken fatally ill at a mammoth
party he gave to celebrate the coming of the new century,
Wells himself dashed over the roads of Sussex to help a
fellow author in distress.*

There was a bicycle in the place and my last clear
memory of that fantastic Brede House party is riding
out of the cold skirts of a wintry night into a drizzling
dawn along a wet road to call up a doctor in Rye.

ibid.

*Wells liked to include others in his cycling enthusiasm;
George Gissing was one.*

I tried to make him a cyclist ... but he was far too
nervous and excitable to ride. It was curious to see
this well-built Viking, blowing and funking as he
hopped behind his machine. 'Get on to your ironmongery', said I. He mounted, wabbled a few yards,
and fell off shrieking with laughter. 'Ironmongery', he
gasped. 'Oh, riding on ironmongery' and lay in the
grass at the roadside, helpless with mirth.

ibid.

Gissing himself took a more optimistic view of his efforts.

Terribly hot for cycling. I can now ride perfectly with one hand, waving the other wildly, or even extracting things from pocket. Fly in the eye has happened, and been overcome without pause.

Gissing to Wells, 16 July 1898.
Gissing and Wells Correspondence, 1961

The cycling craze caught on even with the staidest of writers. Henry James was telling a friend on 4 February 1896:

I must (deride me not) be somewhere where I can, without disaster, bicycle.

The Letters of Henry James, 1920

And Leo Tolstoy, over at Yasnaya Polyana, was learning, at the age of 67, to ride a bicycle. It was March 1895 and he had been presented with a bicycle by the Moscow Society of Velocipede Lovers. While his children admired his skill his disciples were doubtful about the ethics.

I don't know why I like it. Chertkov is offended and finds fault with me for this, but I keep doing it and am not ashamed. On the contrary, I feel that I am entitled to my share of natural light-heartedness, that the opinion of others has no importance, and that there is nothing wrong in enjoying oneself simply, like a boy.

From the Diary of Leo Tolstoy, quoted in
Henri Troyat, *Tolstoy,* 1968

Thomas Hardy was also well past his prime when he took up cycling. With his wife, Emma, an even keener cyclist, he pedalled to Bristol, Gloucester, Poole and Weymouth. He visited friends, such as Meredith and Swinburne, on his bicycle. In the autumn of 1898 Rudyard Kipling visited Hardy in Dorset and they cycled about the neighbourhood together. For Hardy, indeed, the lanes of Wessex were far more appealing than the streets of London.

I asked an omnibus conductor if the young women (who ride recklessly into the midst of the traffic) did not meet with accidents. He said, 'Oh nao; their sex pertects them. We dares not drive over them, wotever they do; and they do jist wot they likes.'

From *The Collected Letters of Thomas Hardy*, 1980

Kipling and his wife, however, were not so fortunate as the young women of the capital.

The Spring of '96 saw us in Torquay. . . . Everybody was learning to ride things called bicycles. In Torquay there was a circular cinder-track where, at stated hours, men and women rode solemnly round and round on them. Tailors supplied special costumes for this sport. Someone . . . had given us a tandem bicycle, whose double steering bars made good dependence for continuous domestic quarrel. On this devil's toast-rack we took exercise, each believing that the other liked it. We even rode it through the idle, empty lanes, and would pass or overtake without upset several carts in several hours. But, one unfortunate day, it skidded, and decanted us on to the road metal. Almost before we had risen from our knees, we made mutual confession of our common loathing of wheels, pushed the Hell-Spider home by hand, and rode it no more.

Rudyard Kipling, *Something of Myself*, 1964

KNIGHTS OF THE
WHIRRING WHEEL

The bicycle found its way into every part of the community. The political world took to it no less eagerly than did writers and men of letters. Gladstone gave it his blessing in 1884.

I consider that physically, morally, and socially, the benefits cycling confers on the men of the present day are almost unbounded, and this belief I endeavour to act up to by heartily welcoming and assisting, as far as in me lies, the many cyclists who came to visit Hawarden and see the grounds. One of the features of my reception in Edinburgh which gave me much pleasure was the escort of some thirty cyclists, who kept pace with the carriage up to the very lodge gates, forming a voluntary bodyguard.

From A. W. Rumney, *A Host of Cycling Years*, 1935

But Gladstone was not quite so enthusiastic when one of his colleagues, A. J. Balfour, arrived at Hawarden on his bicycle.

I rode up from the station on my 'bike' – an uninteresting incident in itself, but amusing in that it shocked the Old Man. He thought it unbefitting a First Lord of the Treasury, and chaffed very amusingly about it. He is, and always was, in everything except essentials, a tremendous old Tory, and is peculiarly sensitive in the matter of dignities. ... On Monday Alice and I went off about 10.30 and bicycled down to the station ... Mr G. came full of interest and amusement to see us off.

Balfour to Lady Elcho, 1–2 September 1896.
From A. J. Balfour, *Chapters of Autobiography*, 1930

Cycling became a major pleasure for Balfour but he did not acquire the skill without mishap – he once appeared on the Treasury bench with his arm in a sling and his foot in a slipper. Lord Grey of Fallodon was as devoted to country life as he was to politics and the bicycle enabled him to enjoy the pleasures of the country. He took his wife, Dorothy, when she was an invalid, in a trailer attached to his bicycle.

I go out a good deal at Fallodon; I took my bicycle over the moorland road from North Charlton and went to the top of Ross Camp one day: a year ago I trailed Dorothy over that road and round by Chillingham and Bellshill. This year too it was a beautiful day and I heard wonderful bird sounds, the spring notes of golden plovers and above all of curlews, as different from their autumn notes as the song of birds is from their chirp, and the sun was glorious and the whole view full of light.

> Lord Grey to Mrs Creighton, 17 April 1906.
> From Edward Grey, *Twenty-Five Years*, 1925

On occasion the bicycle played a part in politics. One Sunday in June 1895 Arthur Balfour was a guest of Lady Jersey at Osterley.

All at once a very hot and dusty figure appeared through the little gate near the portico and revealed itself as Schomberg – commonly called 'Pom' – McDonnell, then Lord Salisbury's Private Secretary. I went to meet him, offering tea, dinner, or whatever hospitality he preferred. All he would say in breathless and very serious tones was 'Give me an egg beat up in brandy and find me Arthur Balfour'.

The desired refreshment and the statesman were produced in due course. It appeared on further inquiry that Mr McDonnell had bicycled from Hatfield to London in search of Mr Balfour, and not finding him in Carlton Gardens had pursued him to Osterley.

... We were not allowed to know the message till next morning when the papers came with the thrilling announcement, 'Resignation of the Government!'

Countess of Jersey, *Fifty-One Years of Victorian Life*, 1923

Sometimes a politician would find the bicycle useful for quite different purposes. In the first week of December 1898, at a crucial stage in the political crisis which led to the Boer War, Alfred Milner, the British pro-consul in South Africa, took off for a six-day cycling trip with his mistress, who had rooms in Brixton.

In most beautiful weather we rode by the Devil's Punch Bowl from Milford to Liphook, taking a late lunch at the Royal Hants Hotel and reaching Liphook just at sunset. It was really a wonderful day, more like mild autumn than winter, and the view from the top of Hindhead splendid.

Milner's Diary, 8 December 1898

When he had to return to London in the middle of the holiday he left his bicycle at Vauxhall station, took a cab to his rooms in Duke Street, changed, and an hour later was dining with the Duke of Marlborough at the Hotel Cecil. When the party broke up, Milner walked across Waterloo Bridge, hailed a cab and drove away south of the river.

Thomas Pakenham, *The Boer War*, 1979

The bicycle played its part in the radicalism of the Nineties which led to the formation of the Independent Labour Party and the Labour Party. One of the offshoots of the Clarion *– the newspaper started by Robert Blatchford in 1891 – was the Clarion Cycling Club. At weekends and holidays thousands of men and women would pedal over the hills, arguing, laughing and singing.*

> What men are you who throng
> The dusty road this summer day,
> Riding together, twenty strong
> Uphill and down in bold array,
> As the times of Border fray
> Knights of the whirring wheel are we
> And whither are ye wending, pray?
> We are on the road to Arcady.
>
> Merry cyclists that, with song
> And laughter, pedal onward say
> How, in a world where chains go wrong,
> Where tyres collapse, and screws give way,

Ye still can be so blithe and gay.
Are all your duns at rest, that ye
Can sing and laugh so lightly? Nay,
We are on the road to Arcady.

W. W. Tomlinson, *To Arcady*, 1895

There were some, however, who had their mind on sterner tasks.

Readers of the *Clarion* may or may not care to give up a few bicycle rides to help canvas for the LCC elections.

Sidney Webb, quoted in Laurence Thompson,
Robert Blatchford, 1951

Even for the army, the bicycle had its uses. One army general organized cycling manoeuvres near Brighton on the wet Bank-holiday weekend of August 1900 to explore the potential of cycling riflemen. The large scale exercise was surprisingly successful but there was one unhappy casualty of army protocol.

On the last day of the manoeuvres 2nd Lieut. Clark met with a very serious accident in consequence of his sword becoming entangled in the cycle. In my judgement this accident illustrates the extreme uselessness and danger of the sword as at present worn by cycle officers. I think it ought to be abandoned altogether as a cyclist's weapon.

Major-General F. Maurice, *Report on Cycle Manoeuvres in Brighton District*, 4, 5, 6 *August 1900*

The bicycle was soon incorporated into military discipline but it required several regulations of the Army Council Manual of 1907 to deal with the training of cyclists – grounding, stacking, unstacking, mounting, dismounting.

A cyclist standing with his cycle, with rifle attached to it, will salute with the right hand, as laid down in Section 19, returning the hand to the point of the saddle on the completion of the salute. When at ease, a cyclist, whether mounted or leading his cycle, will salute by coming to attention, and turning his head to the officer he salutes. A party of cyclists on the march will salute on the command Eyes Right, which will be followed by Eyes Front, from the officer or NCO in charge.

Regulation 64, Army Council Manual

The position of the cyclist at attention is the same as that of the dismounted soldier, except that he will grasp the left steering handle with his left hand, and place the right hand at the point of the saddle, elbow to the rear.

Regulation 65, Army Council Manual

Great Times

Smooth down the Avenue glitters the bicycle
Black-stockinged legs under navy-blue serge,
Home and Colonial, Star, International,
Balancing bicycle leant on the verge.

Trace me your wheel-tracks, you fortunate bicycle,
Out of the shopping and into the dark,
Back down the Avenue, back to the pottingshed,
Back to the house on the fringe of the park.

Sir John Betjeman, from *Myfanwy*, 1940

THERE'S A BICYCLE GOING

*In 1898 the bicycle boom broke and while it was no longer
a fashionable toy there was still one group who continued
to feel its thrill. Now each fresh generation of children
grew up to enjoy the delights of the bicycle.*

A bicycle was the thing I wanted most in the world ...
in my mind's eye is a small green bicycle, a boy's
bicycle, complete with all the latest devices, including a
brake front and rear, made like a horse-shoe, not one of
those outmoded models working off the tyre of the
front wheel ... which wore thin and wouldn't hold
you. ...

My eyes caught sight of the green bicycle and in an
instant it was photographed on my mind. It was
propped against the newel-post of the staircase and
somehow reminded me of a little mountain sheep with
curly horns, its head lowered in apology or defence.

The handlebars, turned towards me, were dwarfed by
the great height of the saddle, which pulled out to its
fullest extent ... disclosed a shining tube of steel six
inches long. ... The bicycle was already dearer to me
than anything I possessed ... I pictured myself riding
it through our village street. ... How everyone would
admire it! I couldn't ride a bicycle but I should soon
learn ... up and down the hills I should go, soaring,
floating.

L. P. Hartley, *The Go-Between*, 1953

Learning to ride was a problem for children as well as
adults.

I had been for some time filled with envy of the boys
whom I saw riding into the school grounds on their
bicycles. It gave a pretty opportunity for showing off
when you entered the gateway without holding on to
the handles. I had persuaded my uncle to let me have
one at the beginning of the summer holidays ... I was
determined to learn to ride it by myself and chaps at
school had told me that they had learned in half an
hour. I tried and tried and at last came to the con-
clusion that I was abnormally stupid ... I seemed at
the end of the first morning no nearer to being able to
get on by myself than at the beginning. Next day ... I
tried several times to mount but fell off each time. ...
After I had been doing this for about an hour ... I saw
two people on bicycles coming along the deserted
road. ... As they passed me the woman swerved
violently to my side of the road and, crashing against
me, fell to the ground.

'Oh, I'm sorry,' she said. 'I knew I should fall off the
moment I saw you' ... I said that it didn't matter at
all. ...

'I think bicycling's lovely, don't you?' she said,
looking at my beautiful new machine which leaned

against the stile. 'It must be wonderful to be able to ride well' ...

'It's only a matter of practice,' I said.

Somerset Maugham, *Cakes and Ale,* 1930

My eldest brother, Herbert and I developed very early a passion for bicycling. ... It was before the days of pneumatic tyres and we took the incredibly heavy and clumsy machine out into Lexham Gardens in order to acquire the art of riding. After a few minutes' practice he allowed me to try my hand, or rather legs. The seat was too high for me and I could only just reach the pedals, but he gave me a shove and I went off with great speed along the gutter, such speed indeed that I collided violently with a lamp post and the bicycle split in two, the handlebars and front wheel going in one direction, the back wheel, seat and myself in another.

Leonard Woolf, *Sowing,* 1960

As one generation drifted away to the next, the delight of the bicycle – often a present for Christmas, a birthday, a reward for passing an exam, winning a scholarship, coming 'top' – was a persistent chorus through the decades.

At the end of 1892 the first detachable pneumatic tyre appeared, and a boy could now mend his own puncture by the wayside. Papa took advantage of the occasion to make the most splendid benefaction in history: he gave each of us a new Dunlop-tyred bicycle. ... We lived on those bicycles in the holidays. We rode behind buses up Park Lane, ringing our bell impatiently and then swinging magnificently past them; we darted between hansom cabs: Look at us! Look at us! Did you ever see bicycles like this?

A. A. Milne, *It's Too Late Now,* 1930

At the beginning of that summer term I achieved my first bicycle, which may have been my reward for winning a Senior Scholarship. It was acquired from a boy called Henson for £7.10. ... I had an early accident with my new bicycle when, in taking my arm from the handlebar in order to raise my hat to a lady, I rode the bicycle into a lamp post and buckled the front wheel ... very soon I was able to steer it with both hands off the handlebar. Lightness was the first object for a schoolboy to aim at in a bicycle. To attain this he took off his brakes and his mud-guards, and most unwillingly left on his bell.

'What does your bike weigh?'

'Twenty-two.'

'Mine only weighs twenty-one.'

And the owner of the twenty-two pounder would turn restlessly over and over before he fell asleep that night, racking his brain for some way of reducing the weight of his machine.

Compton MacKenzie, *My Life and Times,* Octave 2, 1936

... there was a bike going second-hand. Four pounds! ... On Sunday the report lay next to Dad's dinner. 'Top!' he said. 'What's pheno-meenal, George?' 'Better than anybody else' said Mam, 'there's a bicycle going'. She looked at me; I went out. When I got back it was settled. ... I learnt to ride with difficulty, having by now a rooted idea that I was physically awkward. ... Then the machine was put away till school (it might wear out). But I did not mind. ...

It was with a guilty pleasure that on the first morning of the summer term I rose nearly an hour later than ever before, and set off at twenty past eight. ... Near Ty Celyn I passed myself last term, toiling along satchel on back, and almost waved. ... At a quarter to four, a quick run to the shed and I was one of the Boys.

I could hardly be clipped round the ankles, being still in knickerbockers, but at least I could kneel, pump, give my tyre the brisk professional thumb-squeeze, and stand with thickly bandied knees to tweak my trousers away where they had ridden up: they hadn't, but the gesture made me feel like a man. ... The ride home was a spin through long summer afternoons ... I was healthy and relaxed; it was a pleasure to be alive. ... As over my saddle the smooth loins slid rhythmically up and down between slumbrous hedgerows, without knowing it I was wheeling through my last unawakened summer.

Emlyn Williams, *George*, 1961

... the bicycle remained my chief symbol of freedom ... it gave me a sense of liberation and mastery as I skimmed along familiar streets, or choosing a wet patch of road practised controlled skids, or pedalled slowly up Craven Hill on a Saturday morning of early summer, breathing the cool, free air and gently elated by a feeling that all time lay before me.

It was from this bicycle, one summer day in 1917 ... that I first caught sight of the enemy. I had just reached the open space opposite Christ Church when, looking up into the sky north-eastwards, I saw aeroplanes with bent back wings flying towards the centre of London. ... I sat on my bicycle, one foot on the kerb, watching the German aeroplanes out of sight.

Cecil Day-Lewis, *The Buried Day*, 1960

... Take me, my Centaur bike, down Linton Road,
Gliding by newly planted almond trees
Where the young dons with wives in tussore clad
Were building in the morning of their lives
Houses for future Dragons. Rest an arm
Upon the post of the allotment path,
Then dare the slope! We choked in our own dust,

The narrowness of the footpath made our speed
Seem swift as light. May-bush and elm flashed by,
Allotment holders turning round to stare,
Potatoes in their hands. Speed-wobble! Help!
And, with the Sturmey-Archer three-speed gear
Safely in bottom, resting from the race
We pedalled round the new mown meadow-grass
By Marston Ferry with its punt and chain . . .

> Sir John Betjeman, *Summoned by Bells*, 1960

For a boy to get a bicycle was a universal delight.

Freewheeling down the escarpment past the unpassing
    horse
Blazoned in chalk the wind he causes in passing
Cools the sweat of his neck, making him one with the
    sky,
In the heat of the handlebars he grasps the summer
Being a boy and to-day a parenthesis
Between the horizon's brackets; the main sentence
Is to be picked up later but these five minutes
Are all to-day and summer. The dragonfly
Rises without take-off, horizontal,
Underlining itself in a sliver of peacock light.

And glaring, glaring white
The horse on the down moves within his brackets,
The grass boils with grasshoppers, a pebble
Scutters from under the wheel and all this country
Is spattered white with boys riding their heat-wave,
Feet on a narrow plank and hair thrown back

And a surf of dust beneath them. Summer, summer –
They chase it with butterfly nets or strike it into the
    deep
In a little red ball or gulp it lathered with cream
Or drink it through closed eyelids; until the bell

Left-right-left gives his forgotten sentence
And reaching the valley the boys must pedal again
Left-right-left but meanwhile
For ten seconds more can move as the horse in the
    chalk
Moves unbeginningly calmly
Calmly regardless of tenses and final clauses
Calmly unendingly moves.

Louis MacNeice, The Cyclist, 1959

Climbing from Merthyr through the dew of August
    mornings
When I was a centaur-cyclist, on the skills of wheels
I'd loop past The Storey Arms, past steaming lorries
Stopped for flasks of early tea, and fall into
    Breconshire.
A thin road under black Fan Frynych – which keeps
    its winter
Shillings long through spring – took me to the Senni
    valley.

That was my plenty, to rest on the narrow saddle
Looking down on the farms, letting the simple noises
Come singly up. It was there I saw a ring-ousel
Wearing the white gash of his mountains; but every
Sparrow's feather in that valley was rare, golden,
Perfect. It was Eden fourteen miles from home.

Leslie Norris, from A Small War, 1974

Most weekends when the weather was good enough I
used to go cycling in the mountains, usually the Brecon
Beacons or the Black Mountains near the Hereford-
shire border. At that time when I was about fifteen
I used to belong to the Youth Hostel Association, and
so did Del Wellington and Charlie Bond, my friends.
... We knew all the hostels within possible cycling
distance of our homes although we rarely used them.
Del's father had given us a heavy tent, already old, and

we preferred to lug this about with us. We must have looked very odd on our three decrepit cycles – mine was rescued from the scrap yard and restored with loving care and some curious home-made fittings – all our strange equipment tied about us. Del always carried the tent on his bike, its bulk of canvas folded in an awkward sausage beneath his crossbar. It was so big that he had to ride bowlegged. We had great times. I remember camping near the foot of a waterfall. We hadn't meant to stay overnight, but we'd been attracted by the voice of the water, had pushed our bikes over a wet meadow towards the stream, and followed it up about four hundred yards until we reached the water-fall. . . . That year we got away as often as we could. Perhaps it was a natural restlessness, the wish to see over the next hill, and the next; perhaps we realized that time was already beginning to run out for us, that there were responsibilities we would have to recognise, as well as the attractions of more sophisticated and less perfect pleasures.

Leslie Norris, *Slidings,* 1974

I'd always wanted a bike. Speed gave me a thrill. Malcolm Campbell was my bigshot – but I'd settle for a two-wheeled pushbike. I'd once borrowed my cousin's and gone down Balloon House Hill so quick I passed a bus. . . .

The next three evenings, for it was well into summer, I rode a dozen miles out into the country, where fresh air smelt like cow-dung and the land was coloured different, was wide open and windier than in streets: marvellous. It was like a new life starting up, as if till then I'd been tied by a mile-long rope round the ankle to home. Whistling along lanes I planned trips to Skeggy, wondering how many miles I could make in a whole day. If I pedalled like mad, bursting my lungs for fifteen hours I'd reach London where I'd never been: it was like sawing through the bars in clink.

Alan Sillitoe, *The Bike*, 1959

On he jumped and into the road he tore. An old woman with a cow on a tether, a man in a cart, a little girl standing in a door, they all gave him a salute of some kind. A lovely summer morning, with the clean, fine light of the highlands, an invigorating morning with a slight breeze, and into it he tore head down like one escaping in a mad race. . . . In the distance he could now see a lad like himself. Soon he was up behind him and, in a flash, was past.

The boy let out a yell. Iain eased up, turned his head and laughed.

They cycled wheel by wheel. . . . Soon they rounded a bend and saw three cyclists ahead, two girls and a lad, also making for High School after the weekend at home. As they drew nearer, they heard one of the girls singing the song 'Mairi Bran' to a gay rhythm that kept time to her pedalling feet. . . . Iain stood on the pedals and, driving forward full tilt, caught the singing girl's saddle behind and swept her on. She let out a scream. The girl and lad who were a few yards in front turned their heads and the lad swerved. In a moment all four were in collision and thrown off their bikes. Iain landed on his back in the ditch. . . . Iain's face broke in a hard grin as he slowly took the kit-bag from his back. Inside the egg-box was disaster. As he hunted out each yellowed mess of shell and paper and dropped it in the ditch, Angus started laughing.

'Oh, Iain!' said Mary, but she started to laugh, too, in nervous relief.

Neil Gunn, *The Drinking Well*, 1956

The Bike was gold
With silvery lining.
Up it rose
Along the sleeping, winding hill,
As it sang its tune
As it went along the path,
Twisting and curving,
Up and down,
In and out.
The rider
Sat crouched in the saddle
Excited about his first ride
On his bike.

From David Holbrook, *English in Australia Now*, 1973

Before I was sixteen I had many bicycles. . . . But the thing about my bicycles that I want to remember is the way I rode them, what I thought while I rode them, and the music that came to me. . . .

I rode them with speed and style. I found out a great deal about style from riding them. Style in writing, I mean. Style in everything. I did not ride for pleasure. I rode to get somewhere. . . . I mean I rode to get somewhere myself. . . .

A bike can be an important appurtenance of an important ritual. Moving the legs evenly and steadily soon brings home to the bike-rider a valuable knowledge of pace and rhythm, and sensible respect for timing and the meeting of a schedule.

Out of rhythm come many things, perhaps all things. The physical action compels action of another order – action of mind, memory, imagination, dream, hope, order and so on. The physical action also establishes a deep respect for grace, seemliness, effectiveness, power with ease, naturalness and so on. The action of the imagination brings home to the bicycle-rider the limitlessness of the potential in all things.

William Saroyan, *The Bicycle Rider in Beverley Hills,* 1971

THE TWO-WHEELED FRIEND

From childhood to adolescence the bicycle is a friend, a solace in trouble, a sharer in happiness.

> The crimped clouds swim full low
> Over the long chalk breast.
> The cold wind bodes of snow
> As it blows me along to the West.
>
> Bowl over, bowl over, Bicycle wheel!
> Who feels what I feel?
> I'm no sad winter's guest!
> On the road I'm my best
> Full of zest!
> Love's my lode.
>
> Bad weather's no crime
> In the mid-winter time,
> Though there's mud under tyre
> Or it rain or it blow
> Or the water's spell-crossed,

Or come whirligig snow,
Our young blood's at the prime,
There's no sight like the rime,
There's no hush like the frost.

Bowl over, bowl over Bicycle wheel!
There's some life in cold steel
When you're urging amain,
Joints astir,
Frame astrain,
Flowing chain,
Spokes awhirr!

Edmund Vale, *Cycle Song,* 1924

Pink may, double may, dead laburnum
Shedding an Anglo-Jackson shade
Shall we ever, my staunch Myfanwy,
Bicycle down to North Parade?
Kant on the handle-bars, Marx in the saddlebag,
Light my touch on your shoulder-blade.

Sir John Betjeman, *Myfanwy at Oxford,* 1940

I took a whole week off immediately before the Tripos ... in order to be in perfect training for the battle with the papers. I spent the week by myself bicycling among the Yorkshire castles and abbeys.

G. M. Trevelyan, *An Autobiography,* 1949

T. E. Lawrence, when a student at Jesus College, Oxford, went on a bicycle tour in France. He wrote to his mother on 23 July 1908:

For myself I am riding very strongly and feel very fit on my diet of bread, milk, and fruit (peaches (best) 3 a l*d.*): apricots 5 or 6 a l*d.* if very special: cherries don't count) I wish you were here. I begin on two pints of milk and bread & supplement with fruit to taste till evening, when more solid stuff is consumed. One eats a lot when riding for a week on end at my pace. My day begins early (it's fearfully hot at mid-day) there is usually a château to work at from 12.0 to 2.0 and then hotel at 7 or 8.0. I have no time for sight-seeing; indeed sometimes I wonder if my thesis is to be written this November or next, I find myself composing pages and phrases as I ride.

From Aigues Mortes he telephoned to Dunlop in Paris for a new tyre.

... since then all has gone like a marriage bell in the way of punctures, and I am generally happy. The cost was, however, immense with telephoning, carriage, fitting etc it cost nearly 20s. ... truly the Auvergne is a wondrous district, but *not* one for a cycle. ... From Le Puy I rode up for ten miles more (oh dear 'twas hot! ...) I got to the top at last, had 15 miles of up and down to St Somebody-I-don't want to meet again and then a rush down 4000 feet to the Rhône. 'Twas down a valley, the road carved out of the side of the precipice, and most gloriously exciting!

The Letters of T. E. Lawrence, 1913

And the bicycle has often played its part in love. There is even something sexual about the machine itself.

> The line is man
> The circle woman.
> Bisexual bicycle
> carry us on the diamond frame
> on the sounds of the wheels
> by the silent work
> of cable chain and gear
> to deeper distances.
> Link us to our double selves.
>
> Peter Cummings, *Going Bicycle,* 1979

Oh would I could subdue the flesh
   Which sadly troubles me!
And then perhaps could view the flesh
As though I never knew the flesh
   And merry misery.

To see the golden hiking girl
   With wind about her hair,
The tennis-playing, biking girl,
The wholly-to-my-liking girl,
   To see and not to care.

At sundown on my tricycle
   I tour the Borough's edge,
And icy as an icicle
See bicycle by bicycle
   Stacked waiting in the hedge.

Get down from me! I thunder there.
   You spaniels! Shut your jaws!
Your teeth are stuffed with underwear,
Suspenders torn asunder there
   And buttocks in your paws!

Oh whip the dogs away my Lord
   They make me ill with lust.
Bend bare knees down to pray, my Lord,
Teach sulky lips to say, my Lord,
   That flaxen hair is dust.

                  Sir John Betjeman, *Senex*, 1940

H. G. Wells describes a visit to his divorced wife, Isabel.

I bicycled to the place [a poultry farm at Twyford] and
found her amidst green things and swarming creatures
depending upon her. We spent a day together at
Virginia Water.... Suddenly I found myself overcome by the sense of our separation. I wanted fantastically to recover her. I implored her for the last time in

vain. Before dawn the house had become unendurable for me. I got up and dressed and went down to find my bicycle and depart. She heard me moving about ... and she came down ... I gave way to a wild storm of weeping. I wept in her arms like a disappointed child and then suddenly pulled myself together and went out into the summer dawn and mounted my bicycle and wandered off southward into a sunlit intensity of perplexity and frustration, unable to understand the peculiar keenness of my unhappiness.

H. G. Wells, *Experiment in Autobiography,* 1934

I went out bicycling one afternoon and suddenly, as I was riding along a country road, I realized that I no longer loved Alys. . . .

Bertrand Russell, *Autobiography,* 1967

He dropped down the hills on his bicycle. The roads were greasy so he had to let it go. He felt a pleasure as the machine plunged over the second, steeper drop in the hill. Here goes! he said. It was risky, because of the curve in the darkness at the bottom, and because of the brewer's waggons with drunken waggoners asleep. His bicycle seemed to fall beneath him, and he loved it. Recklessness is almost a man's revenge on his woman. He feels he is not valued so he will risk destroying himself to deprive her altogether.

D. H. Lawrence, *Sons and Lovers,* 1913

> Miss Gee looked up at the starlight
>   And said: 'Does anyone care
> That I live in Clevedon Terrace
>   On one hundred pounds a year?'
>
> She dreamed a dream one evening
>   That she was the Queen of France
> And the vicar of Saint Aloysius
>   Asked Her Majesty to dance.

But a storm blew down the palace,
    She was biking through a field of corn,
And a bull with the face of the Vicar
    Was charging with lowered horn.

She could feel his hot breath behind her,
    He was going to overtake;
And the bicycle went slower and slower
    Because of that back-pedal brake . . .

W. H. Auden, from *Miss Gee,* 1976

The bicycle is sometimes an outlet for other passions, and a
friend in time of trouble.

He had acquired a rust-eaten bicycle and increasingly
took to pedalling into the countryside to dull his pain
with the monotonous grind at the worn out pedals and
the peacefully bitter silence of the fields and woods.
Heedless of route or destination he would turn his
handlebars at random; when night fell he lit his lamps
and mournfully pushed on. It was a powerful drug, and
he turned eagerly to it whenever his daily toil allowed.

John Wain, *Hurry on Down,* 1953

I had it all wrong from the start
about four-letter words. I thought
they were big words with four letters.

Sure, I thought about being wrong.
I kept it quiet, cobweb quiet,
like our house, even our garage.

All but the shed where I kept my bike.
I looked for a place
to hear these words, all of them,

Before someone tried to tell me
where this one belonged and that
one didn't. Leaning streamlined

Over the handlebars, I heard them
in the tire's lick and spin. Faster,
tearing all out down a hill, hunched

Under the wind, blinking at the rain,
I yelled every four-letter word I knew,
yelled them until they were as real

As the hill, yelled them until I
broke them in my throat and they were
just words spinning in the spokes.

Peter Sears, *Four Letter Words*

Under the dawn I wake my two-wheel friend.
Shouting in bed my mother says to me,
'Mind you don't clatter it going downstairs!'
I walk him down he springing step to step:
those tyres he has, if you pat him flat-handed
he'll bounce your hand. I mount with an air
and as light a pair of legs as you'll encounter,
slow into Sunday ride out of the gates,
roll along asphalt, press down on the pedals,
speeding   fearless,
     ring,
       ring,
         ring
get clear of Moscow, frighten a one-eyed cock
with a broken tail, lend a boy a spanner
(his hair a white mane) drink brown kvas
passing Kuntsevo in a cloud of dust,
lean up against the kvas tank (warmed with sun
hot on my back). The girl who's serving gives me
a handful of damp change from a damp hand,
won't say her name, 'You're artful all you boys . . .'
I smile 'So long . . .'

             Yevgeny Yevtushenko, from *On a Bicycle,* 1962

At half-past seven every morning Mrs Thurlow
pushed her great rusty bicycle down the hill; at six
every evening she pushed it back. Loaded, always, with
grey bundles of washing, oilcans, sacks, cabbages,
bundles of old newspapers, boughs of wind-blown
wood, and bags of chicken food, the bicycle could never
be ridden. It was a vehicle of necessity. Her relation-
ship to it was that of a beast to a cart. Slopping along
beside it, flat heavy feet pounding painfully along under
mudstained skirts, her face and body ugly with humpy
angles of bone, she was like a beast of burden. . . .
Grasping its handles, she felt a sense of security and
fortitude. The notion of walking without it, helplessly,

[83]

in the darkness, was unthinkable. ... The familiar smooth handlebars hard against her hands had the living response of other hands. They brought back her sense of reality.

H. E. Bates, *The Ox*, 1939

MAN ON A BICYCLE

One can take an altogether more serious view of the bicycle. It can be a dialectical symbol of man's aspirations.

Lucretius could not credit centaurs;
Such bicycle he deemed asynchronous.
'Man superannuates the horse;
Horse pulses will not gear with ours.'

Johnson could see no bicycle would go;
'You bear yourself, and the machine as well.'
Gennets for germans sprang not from Othello,
And Ixion rides upon a single wheel.

Courage. Weren't strips of heart culture seen
Of late mating two periodicities?
Could not Professor Charles Darwin
Graft annual upon perennial trees?

William Empson, *Invitation to Juno*, 1969

Then there is the question of efficiency.

Man on a bicycle can go three or four times faster than the pedestrian, but uses five times less energy in the process. He carries one gram of his weight over a kilometre of flat road at an expense of only 0.15 calories. The bicycle is the perfect traducer to match man's metabolic energy to the independence of locomotion. Equipped with this tool, man out-strips the efficiency of not only all machines, but all other animals as well.

Ivan Illitch, *Energy and Equity*, 1974

[84]

From the early days the bicycle has been used as a record-breaker – the fastest speed, the furthest distance, the oddest journey. In 1884 Thomas Stevens rode round the world on a high bicycle: it took him two and a half years. The titles of dusty volumes record other exploits:

Bonn to Metz on a Boneshaker, Land's End to John o'Groats on a Tricycle, Across Siberia on a Bicycle, London to Peking Awheel.

... cycling is easily the most satisfactory way of touring. ... You are in intimate contact with the countryside and its people. You are accepted more readily as one of themselves. You can stay in village inns where interesting conversation is available far more readily than in grand hotels. You can keep up a steady fifty or sixty miles a day without effort – this involves only five or six hours' actual cycling affording ample leisure to look around. ... I now travelled alone – the perfect way for he who would learn. ... And I *had* a companion – my bicycle. I christened him George. ... In the summer of 1937 I set off on the most ambitious of my journeys with George – to ride across Europe to Russia. I went from Holland into Germany where the obvious and deliberate stimulation of war mentality caused me great concern. Yet even Nazi Germany had its comedies. In the Hartz Mountains I stumbled across a German nudist camp. Naturally its occupants *were* nude – but their leaders proudly wore a Nazi swastika armlet!

Bernard Newman, *Speaking from Memory,* 1960

Some cycle tourists prefer to travel in groups.

The Bradford folk have always gone streaming out to the moors. In the old days ... everybody went on enormous walks. ... Now they were in gangs of either hikers or bikers. ... These youngsters looked too

[85]

much as if they were consciously taking exercise ... and I remember wondering exactly what pleasure they were getting from the surrounding country, as they never seemed to lift their heads from their handle-bars, but went grimly on like racing cyclists. They might just as well, I thought, be going round and round the city. But perhaps they call an occasional halt, and then take in all the beauty with a deep breath.

J. B. Priestley, *English Journey,* 1934

The most professional cyclist is the racing cyclist. Sometimes he races on a track.

The blast of the pistol swept off the Blue Riband riders and there were shouts and curses and skirmishes and spills, even before all the cyclists had cleared the starting line. The crowd broke into a roar again and everyone seemed calling on his favourite to break away. ... After twenty laps the field thinned out a good deal ... Leon had moved up near the head of the race. ... The cyclists sped round and the race was getting hot. ... The excitement reached fever pitch. At the front there was a group of eight and the rest did not seem to be seriously in the race ... Leon was ready to swoop. ... To him Prestor was the only man who still looked strong. Prestor was his friend but really he had no friend, no, not in this game. ... His front wheel was so close to Prestor's that they were almost rubbing. He was feeling good. ... He was feeling strong and brutal. ... The shouting was mad now and he heard the crowd calling on him, and the people on the edge of the track were wild with excitement. ... He moved into the wind now, taking the fifty-ninth lap and the group was bunching up closer and every man was marking the other. ... He felt as though aflame. ... The pace was getting blistering. He was desperate. ... He had to make the Wasp fly now. He had to make the Wasp talk! He got off the saddle and hammered with everything he had in him. Half a lap to go and Guaracara Park was a shouting, screaming din. . . . Now they took the home straight. Leon's head hung forward and he pushed and pounded until the tissues of his belly felt as though they would be ripped away. He was in the very last of his strength. His face twisted in agony, and his lips were skinned, and were white with the dust, and he rocked and jerked the bike, and now his tyre found a little edge in front and as he struggled to maintain it chaos broke over the grounds . . . as the dust kicked, and the flag went up, he was overwhelmed and he wept.

Michael Anthony, *The Games Were Coming*, 1963

Sometimes he races long distance. The most famous of all is the Tour de France, ridden every June over 2,500 miles in twenty-four days.

The Director of the Tour ceremoniously raises his chrome-plated scissors and with a flourish and a smile cuts the ribbon. Hundreds of throats yell, '*Allez*', timing devices are started and we move forward groping for our toe-clip straps and slipping into higher gears. The pace quickens and already the regimented lines of one hundred and twenty coloured jerseys are beginning to mix. . . . There can't be anything much harder than cycling at competition speeds over the highest mountain roads in mid-summer. There's no way to stop or ease the sweating; my pores seem literally to open like floodgates. . . . Scenery is something you can't take in. It's always there but you never see it, and neither do you notice the countless thousands of spectators whom you must pass. . . . You can never be at ease and never let your mind wander for long from the race. Always you're too tired, too hot, too demoralized, too thirsty. The limit of your world is between the leading and tailing riders, and always there's the road in front, winding, ascending, dropping away ... I'm nearly out of water and so take only an occasional sip to keep my mouth moist. Then, to make matters worse, I drop the bottle as I pull it from its cage on the handlebars. My hands are slippery with sweat and the bottle shoots from my grip like a wet piece of soap and clatters away into the gutter. The dormant boil seems to hear the clattering and takes it as a cue to start throbbing. ... Today's stage is the shortest in the race. It is in fact only twenty-one kilometres ... Mont Ventoux – The Giant of Provence – is an extinct volcano, and the road that winds to its summit climbs to five thousand feet in that twenty-one kilometres ... it's not the gradient or the length of the climb that makes the mountain so infamous. It's the heat ... in June it becomes a dust-choked, rock-strewn, shadeless wasteland, to be pounded up in intense heat from a sun that hangs up there in a cloudless sky like a polished brass gong. ... The limits of our world are made up of aching limbs and hammering head, creaking cycles with frames and bars which strain and whip under our efforts, sweat and pain and gradient and furnacelike heat ... again it's up and up and up until I think I must have died and am in an everlasting climbing purgatory ... I suddenly become aware of a lot of things ... I'm aware of the crowds and of the *Arrivée* banner stretched across the road ahead. Before we reach it I stop pedalling, and as it passes above me I feel I've just ridden through the gates of paradise.

Richard Hurne, *The Yellow Jersey*, 1973

The hero-worship evoked by such races takes on a religious tone.

A recess at the back of the Palma Cycling Club provides a shrine for one of their members killed on a mountain road during the Tour of Spain – his pedals and shoes hung up beneath a St Christopher, with candles perpetually burning.

Robert Graves, *A Bicycle in Majorca*, 1958

The most original cycle race captured the religious symbolism.

Barabbas, slated to race, was scratched ... Pilate gave the send off. Jesus got away to a good start ... but he had a flat right away. A bed of thorns punctured the whole circumference of his front tire. ... There are fourteen turns in the difficult Golgotha course. Jesus took his first spill at the third turn. His mother, who was in the stands, became alarmed. ...

The second spill came at the seventh turn on some slippery pavement. Jesus went down for the third time at the eleventh turn, skidding on a rail. ... The deplorable accident familiar to us all took place at the twelfth turn. Jesus was in a dead heat at the time with the thieves. We know that he continued the race airborne – but that is another story.

Alfred Jarry, *The Passion Considered as an Uphill Bicycle Race*, 1969

And there was a race of a different kind when Mark Brayne, the BBC Berlin correspondent, cycled with his wife by tandem along the road – 138 miles – between West Berlin and Hamburg.

It's a long way, through Communist territory, it's busy and often narrow and worst of all, the East Germans insist that you reach the other end by nightfall. . . . Midsummer is the only time of the year when the days are long enough. . . . We set off from home just before four in the morning on the third longest day of the year, 24 June – with some trepidation. . . . Our route began in a little East German village, just west of the barbed wire, tank-traps and electrified fencing that isolate West Berlin from surrounding East Germany. . . . We were already half way by nine o'clock. The countryside was overwhelmingly beautiful, unspoilt more by default than by design. The roads are still flanked by huge chestnuts, oaks and lime trees. . . . The villages seem hardly touched since the war – old half-timbered houses and church after church, 26 in all. . . . In the early morning we encountered several locals clanking home from the dairy on ancient bicycles with empty milk-churns hanging from the handle-bars. The frustrating thing was that, like cars along the transit routes, we weren't allowed to leave the main road. You can see picturesque villages beckoning across the fields, lakes waiting to be picnicked beside, stately homes from Germany's Prussian past that you know you can't visit. . . . The weather turned, around tea-time, and we crossed into West Germany in pouring rain, half an hour before sunset. Altogether $15\frac{1}{2}$ hours travelling, although a good third of that was spent eating and resting, plus half an hour lost on the inevitable puncture repair.

The Listener, 5 July 1979

BEARD AND BICYCLE

*The golden age of the spinning wheel is now no more than a
nostalgic memory.*

Alas, how many years have flown
    Since first your silvery note I sounded
And on a cycle of my own
    First o'er the bumps in boyhood bounded,
And felt, like Icarus, the delight
Of suddenly acquiring flight.

The roads were peaceful then; no noise
    More strident than your ring intruded,
And bells of other little boys
    Who also cycled (as a few did),
And those of elder people who
Sedately pedalled two-by-two.

But the inventive brain of man,
    As restless as the winds that fan it,
Is always making some new plan
    To work commotion on our planet;
Especially if it thinks we need
Devices for increasing speed . . .

When in the future I retire
    (So runs my fanciful reflection)
And find some land of heart's desire
    Where everything will be perfection,
Motors shall vanish like a dream
And cycles be once more supreme.

Guy Boas, from *To a Bicycle Bell*, 1933

I'm pedalling in to work
thinking about God's works.
He's pedalling in to work.
Old man and old grid.
Not far to go now
to the end of the ride.

Look at him, weaving
slower and slower, in and out
of the hating, snarled-up traffic.
He's old and slow
but skilful;
he's doing no harm
but patient
under unjust rebuke . . .

Come, friend, let's go.
The lights are green.
Let's away
to the green places.
And Gabriel will not hoot us
on a hectoring horn.
I hear his bell,
blinkling, brinkling.
And thy rood
and thy verge
shall lead us
safely
under the ring roads.

> Peter Sizer, from *Old Man on a Bicycle*, 1977

And each new generation of cyclists has learnt to carry on the guerrilla war for survival against the internal combustion engine and its relentless masters.

I avoid the general hills and vales of lower New York by cycling along the upland ridge, which is Eighth Avenue up to Thirty-fourth Street. . . . One thing to look out for is De Martino's fish truck, which is invariably parked diagonally to the curb on the east side of Eighth just above Sixteenth Street, tending to force you out into the taxi stream. . . . If a bus shows up, I have found a crisply delivered 'Watch it, pal' to be a relatively effective admonition when you are parallel with the vehicle, and holding your breath the best defense when you are behind it. Holding your breath is not a bad idea in general. You will find that this not only protects your lungs from pollution but improves stamina and, if carefully controlled, leads to creative hallucinating. . . . Another thing to look out for is pot-holes. . . . You must keep your eyes on the terrain at all times. The rest of the time you must watch out for parked cars. Yes, *parked* cars! There is a special brand of loony in New York who likes to sit in his car and watch in his rearview mirror for a cyclist. Here comes one now! Time to open the front door and get out and stretch. These people like it best if the bus parade is just coming up on your left flank. . . .

New Yorker, 11 July 1977

Cycling in New York in the Nineties was a very different matter.

Josephine and I rode out on our wheels. . . . We started at 2.30 in the afternoon while it was still very warm, wheeled swiftly over the smooth asphalt of the Boulevard (as Broadway is called from 59th Street to 125th Street). At 108th Street we turned westward to the Riverside Drive where on good hard roads we skirted the Hudson where it is most magnificent. This road stops with Claremont, an old Livingston manor house, now used as a fashionable inn and a favourite resort for riders, drivers and bicyclists. Eastward we turned, back into the boulevard. Down a bad grade we picked our way to 125th Street, where a long ascent began. . . . At the top of the grade, we sat on a big boulder and our watches told us we had travelled an hour, while the cyclometers recorded seven miles. In our saddles again we spun down that part of Broadway which is called King's Bridge. Near the bottom the road was being repaired; in the soft dirt Josephine fell off her wheel. She was not hurt but we took to the side-walk, rolling along at a good pace till we came to King's Bridge, the river crossing and the village of Kingsbridge. Without a halt we rode slowly through the sleepy hamlet, and leaving Broadway for the day we crossed the railroad tracks (New York Central) into Riverdale Avenue. It was a hard climb and the eleven miles we had accomplished were telling on Josephine.

The Letters of Lincoln Steffens, 5 May 1895

You may never get to Heaven on Roller Skates but some believe that the Bicycle can take you to Utopia.

Socialism can only come riding on a bicycle.

José Antonio Viera-Gallo of Chile

As an alternative to technocratic disaster I propose the vision of a convivial society. . . . Transportation beyond bicycle speeds demands power inputs from the environment. . . . The energy used up in the United States for the sole purpose of driving vehicles built to accelerate beyond bicycle speed would suffice to add auxiliary motors to about twenty times that many vehicles for people all over the world who want to move at bicycle speeds and do not or cannot push the pedals because they are sick or old. . . . Simply on the basis of equal distribution on a world-wide scale, speed above those attained by bicycles could be ruled out. . . .

Ivan Illitch, *Tools for Conviviality,* 1973

A London doctor who took to doing his rounds on a bicycle because it was more pleasant, healthier, more economical of energy and did not pollute the air, decided that the future might well belong to Cycling Man.

Our descendants will look back on a time of some difficulty for *Homo Sapiens*. . . . An originally privileged subgroup of the species failed to adapt. They came to believe that they could not move any distance unless they were carried, either by their cars or some other propulsive aid. They ceased to do any significant muscular work, and by one of those strange twists of history they became in the end the prisoners of the machines which were to have set them free. . . . This pitiable creature was known at first as *Homo vehiculo constrictus* but . . . he came to be called simply *Homo constrictus*. . . . All future races of mankind descended from the other more active subgroup – *Homo se propellens*. This advanced human primate was clever, keen, and cultured. His archetype in many societies was the cross-country runner. He walked or went on a bicycle, and he survived.

Ronald E. Williams, *British Medical Journal*, 4 October 1975

The bicycle may be a means to the good life for those who ride them but not for those who make them.

The minute you stepped out of the factory gates you thought no more about your work. But the funniest thing was that neither did you think about work when you were standing at your machine. You began the day by cutting and drilling steel cylinders with care, but gradually your actions became automatic and you forgot all about the machine and the quick working of your arms and hands and the fact that you were cutting and boring and rough-threading to within limits of only five-thousandths of an inch. The noise of motor trolleys passing up and down the gangway and the excruciating din of flying and flapping belts slipped out of your consciousness after perhaps half an hour, without affecting the quality of the work you were turning out. ... If your machine was working well – the motor smooth, stops tight, jigs good – and you spring your actions into a favourable rhythm you became happy. You went off into pipe-dreams for the rest of the day. And in the evening when admittedly you would be feeling as though your arms and legs had been stretched to breaking point on a torture-rack, you stepped out into a cosy world of pubs and noisy tarts that would one day provide you with the raw material for more pipe-dreams as you stood at your lathe.

Alan Sillitoe, *Saturday Night and Sunday Morning*, 1958

The bicycle has acquired an eccentric air.

His eyes followed the high figure in homespun, beard and bicycle, a listening woman at his side. Coming from the vegetarian. Only weggebobbles and fruit. Don't eat a beefsteak. If you do the eyes of that cow will pursue you through all eternity. They say it' healthier. Wind and watery though. Her stockings all loose over her ankles. I detest that: so tasteless they are. Those literary etherial people all. Dreamy, cloudy, symbolistic. Esthetes they are.

James Joyce, *Ulysses*, 1937

For some cycling has become a cult.

Not for him the flying coat-tails and bare knees of crouched pedallers moving in masses to the coast on Sunday, nor the rusty frame and the bunch of vegetables on the handle-bars of the purely utilitarian cycle. . . . He cycled for pleasure and alone. . . . But he made of cycling more than either a sport or a necessity, a gesture of defiance of all the advancing forces of destruction. He rode with a suggestion of contempt for both car drivers and pedestrians – for him this was the best, the only enjoyable means of transport. It was a cult, not a hobby.

He used his cycle for some impertinent escapades which laid him open to snubs, prohibitions, even penalties. He cycled about London, oblivious of frayed tempers in drivers or police, conforming to traffic regulations as much as he could conform to anything but with an air of *droit de seigneur* which must have been infuriating to hard-pressed motorists. Sitting upright, dressed in elegant town clothes, he would ride down Piccadilly as though it were the drive of his private park. He cycled into the Tower of London and was saluted as a returning officer, he cycled into the grounds of royal palaces and private mansions, calmly to ring at some stone carved entrance and demand to see the building. He cycled up to the doors of the Berkeley or the Dorchester and coolly handed his bicycle to a usually over-tipped and self-important doorman with instructions to look after it while he was dining.

R. Croft-Cooke, *The Wild Hills,* 1966

In America in the Seventies people were suddenly 'into' cycling and taking their machines into the oddest places.

In Marin County, California, the ten-speed became a status symbol.

Bicycling home from the Sausalito ferry that Friday evening, Harvey hung a right into his driveway as usual and narrowly missed a head-on with Angela Stein's BMW 2002. . . . Three other cars that looked familiar were scattered along the block. . . . Harvey walked his bike into the family room and chained it to the wall; not that he was heavily into private property, but anybody who ripped off his Motobecane was going to have to rip off the whole tract house with it. Then he headed for the living room, keeping his Bell helmet on just to be safe.

Cyra McFadden, The Serial, 1977

And in Washington one of the Post *reporters, Carl Bernstein, rode down clues to the Watergate scandal.*

There was a pretty fair bike shop in McLean, and Bernstein drove there to kill a couple of hours and look half-heartedly for a replacement for his beloved Raleigh. But his mind was on Jeb Magruder. He had picked up a profoundly disturbing piece of information that day: Magruder was a bike freak. Bernstein had trouble swallowing the information that a bicycle nut could be a Watergate bugger. And Magruder really was a card-carrying bicycle freak who had even ridden his 10-speed to the White House every day. Nobody would ever steal Jeb Magruder's bike, at least not there. Bernstein knew that, because he had ridden his bike to the White House on July 14 – not the Raleigh, but a Holdsworth that he had had built in London – and as he went through the gate he knew no one would get near it.

Carl Bernstein and Bob Woodward,
All the President's Men, 1974

The simplicity of the bicycle made its impact on the world of art. In 1913 the surrealist artist Marcel Duchamp created an art form called 'readymades', one of which was the front wheel of a bicycle mounted upside down on a kitchen stool where a touch of the hand would set it spinning.

It just came about as a pleasure; something to have in my room the way you have a fire, or a pencil sharpener, except that there was no usefulness. It was a pleasant gadget, pleasant for the movement it gave.

Marcel Duchamp quoted in *The Bride and the Bachelors*,
Calvin Tomkins, 1965

One can go so far as to fall in love with the bicycle itself.

How can I convey the perfection of my comfort on the bicycle, the completeness of my union with her, the sweet responses she gave me at every particle of her frame? I felt that I had known her for many years and that she had known me and that we understood each other utterly. . . .

I passed my hand with unintended tenderness – sensuously indeed – across the saddle. . . . It was a gentle saddle yet calm and courageous. . . . Her saddle seemed to spread invitingly into the most enchanting of all seats while her two handlebars, floating finely with the wild grace of alighting wings, beckoned to me to lend my mastery for free and joyful journeyings, the lightest of light running in the company of the swift ground winds to safe havens far away, the whir of the true front wheel in my ear as it spun perfectly beneath my clear eye and the strong fine back wheel with unadmired industry raising gentle dust on the dry roads. How desirable her seat was, how charming the invitation of her slim encircling handlebars, how unaccountably competent and reassuring her pump resting warmly against her rear thigh.

Flann O'Brien, *The Third Policeman*, 1967

Or at least become heavily entangled.

So I got up, adjusted my crutches and went down to the road where I found my bicycle (I didn't know I had one) in the same place I must have left it. Which enables me to remark that, crippled though I was, I was no mean cyclist, at that period. This is how I went about it. I fastened my crutches to the cross-bar, one on either side, I propped the foot of my stiff leg (I forget which, now they're both stiff) on the projecting front axle, and I pedalled with the other. It was a chainless bicycle, with a free wheel, if such a bicycle exists. Dear bicycle, I shall not call you bike, you were green, like so many of your generation. I don't know why. It is a pleasure to meet it again. ... I pushed and pulled in vain, the wheels would not turn. It was as though the brakes were jammed, and heaven knows they were not, for my bicycle had no brakes.

Samuel Beckett, *Malloy*, 1959

And a bicycle sometimes brings one up against the law.

'My front lamp, constable? Why man, the moon!
    My rear lamp?
Shining there ten yards behind me,
Warm parlour lamplight of the Dish and Spoon!'
But for all my fancy talk, they would have fined me
Had I not set a rather sly half-crown
Winking under the rays of my front lamp;
Goodwill-towards-men disturbed the official frown,
My rear-light beckoned through the evening's damp.

Robert Graves, *A Vehicle, to Wit, a Bicycle*, 1921

One should, in any case, beware. A love affair with a bicycle can get out of hand.

'. . . people who spent most of their natural lives riding iron bicycles over the rocky roadsteads of this parish get their personalities mixed up with the personalities of their bicycles as a result of the interchanging of the atoms of each of them and you would be surprised at the number of people in these parts who nearly are half people and half bicycles.'

I let go a gasp of astonishment that made a sound in the air like a bad puncture. . . .

'When a man lets things go so far that he is half or more than half a bicycle, you will not see so much because he spends a lot of his time leaning with one elbow on walls or standing propped by one foot at kerbstones. Of course there are other things connected with ladies and ladies' bicycles that I will mention to you separately some time. But the man-charged bicycle is a phenomenon of great charm and intensity and a very dangerous article. . . .'

'And what way do these people's bicycles behave? . . .'

'The behaviour of a bicycle that has a high content of humanity', he said, 'is very cunning and entirely remarkable. You never see them moving by themselves but you meet them in the least accountable places unexpectedly. Did you never see a bicycle leaning against the dresser of a warm kitchen when it is pouring outside?'

'I did.'

'Not very far from the fire?'

'Yes.'

'Near enough to the family to hear the conversation?'

'Yes.'

'Not a thousand miles from where they keep the eatables?'

'I did not notice that. You do not mean to say that these bicycles *eat food*?'

'They were never seen doing it, nobody ever caught them with a mouthful of steak. All I know is that the food disappears.'

'What!'

'It is not the first time I have noticed crumbs at the front wheels of some of these gentlemen.'

'All this is a great blow to me. . . .'

'Many a grey hair it has put into my head, trying to regulate the people of this parish. If you let it go too far it would be the end of everything. You would have bicycles wanting votes and they would get seats on the County Council and make the roads far worse than they are for their own ulterior motivation. But against that and on the other hand, a good bicycle is a great companion, there is a great charm about it.'

'How would you know a man has a lot of bicycle in his veins?'

'If his number is over Fifty you can tell it unmistakeably from his walk. He will walk smartly always and never sit down and he will lean against the wall with his elbow out and stay like that all night in his kitchen instead of going to bed. If he walks too slowly or stops in the middle of the road he will fall down in a heap and will have to be lifted and set in motion again by some extraneous party. This is the unfortunate state that the postman has cycled himself into, and I do not think he will ever cycle himself out of it.'

'I don't think I will ever ride a bicycle,' I said.

Flann O'Brien, *The Third Policeman,* 1967

Acknowledgements

Compiling this anthology has been a truly co-operative venture and it represents only a small selection of the many poems, songs, anecdotes, extracts from novels and fragments of autobiography which I have collected and received. I have first to thank personal friends and all those readers of the magazine *Cycletouring* – both in England and Canada – who replied so generously to my appeal for help. I would like to mention each one of them by name but the list is too long to do so. I must, however, give special thanks to John Way, the ex-editor of *Cycletouring*, for giving me access to the archives of the magazine, to Arthur Tapp and Beth Inglis of Sussex University Library, to the staff of the London Library, to George Spater for his continuing help and invaluable suggestions, and, above all, to that inveterate cycling bookseller and bibliophile Douglas Marchant.

The editor and publishers gratefully acknowledge permission to use copyright material in this book:

Michael Anthony: Extract from *The Games Were Coming* (Deutsch 1963).

W. H. Auden: From *The English Auden: Poems, Essays & Dramatic Writings 1927–1939*, edited by Edward Mendelson. Copyright 1940 and renewed 1968 by W. H. Auden. Reprinted by permission of Faber & Faber Ltd. and Random House, Inc.

H. E. Bates: Extract from 'The Ox' from *Thirty-One Selected Tales* (Jonathan Cape Ltd.). Reprinted by permission of Laurence Pollinger Ltd. for the Estate of the late H. E. Bates.

Samuel Beckett: Extract from *Malloy*. Reprinted by permission of Calder & Boyars Ltd., and Grove Press, Inc.

Max Beerbohm: Extract from *Seven Men and Two Others* (Heinemann). Reprinted by permission of Mrs Eva Reichmann.

Carl Bernstein & Bob Woodward: Extract from *All the President's Men* (S & S Enterprises, 1974).

Sir John Betjeman: Extracts from 'Summoned by Bells', 'Senex' and 'Myfanwy at Oxford', all from *Collected Poems*. Reprinted by permission of John Murray (Publishers) Ltd.

Guy Boas: This poem first appeared in *Punch*, 22 Dec. 1926, and is reprinted here by permission of *Punch*.

Mark Brayne: Extract from an article which first appered in *The Listener*, 5 July 1979. Reprinted by permission of the author.

ACKNOWLEDGEMENTS

Richard Church: Extracts from *Over the Bridge*. Reprinted by permission of Laurence Pollinger Ltd. for the Estate of the late Richard Church.

Rupert Croft-Cooke: Extracts from *The Wild Hills*. Reprinted by permission of W. H. Allen & Co. Ltd.

Peter Cummings: From *Bicycle Consciousness*. Reprinted by permission of The Greenfield Review Press, Greenfield Center, N.Y. 12833.

C. Day-Lewis: Extract from *The Buried Day*. Reprinted by permission of Chatto & Windus Ltd. on behalf of the Author's Literary Estate, and A. D. Peters & Co. Ltd.

William Empson: From *Collected Poems*. Copyright 1949, 1977 by William Empson. Reprinted by permission of Chatto & Windus Ltd. and Harcourt Brace Jovanovich, Inc.

F. Scott Fitzgerald & Zelda Fitzgerald: Extract from 'What a Handsome Pair' in *Bits of Paradise*. Reprinted by permission of The Bodley Head and Charles Scribner's Sons.

R. A. Gettman: Extract from *Gissing and Wells Correspondence*, edited by R. A. Gettman. Reprinted by permission of Granada Publishing Ltd.

Robert Graves: 'A Bicycle in Majorca' from *Steps*. 'A Vehicle, to Wit, a Bicycle' first appeared in the *New Statesman*, 16 July 1921. Both reprinted by permission of A. P. Watt Ltd.

Neil Gunn: Extract from *The Drinking Well*. Reprinted by permission of Souvenir Press Ltd.

L. P. Hartley: Extract from *The Go-Between*. Copyright © 1973 the Executors of the late L. P. Hartley. Reprinted by permission of Hamish Hamilton Ltd.

David Holbrook: From *English in Australia Now* (edited by D. Holbrook), by an Australian schoolboy, Robert. Reprinted by permission of Cambridge University Press.

Derek Hudson: Extract from *Munby, Man of Two Worlds* (John Murray 1972/Gambit, USA, 1972). Reprinted by permission of John Murray (Publishers) Ltd.

Richard Hurne: Extract from *The Yellow Jersey*. Reprinted by permission of George Weidenfeld & Nicolson, and Kurt Hellmer for the author.

Ivan Illitch: Extract from *Energy and Equity* (Calder & Boyars). Reprinted by permission of Marion Boyars Publishers Ltd. Extract from *Tools for Conviviality* (1973). Reprinted by permission of Marion Boyars Publishers Ltd. and Harper & Row, Inc.

Alfred Jarry: Extract from *Selected Works of Alfred Jarry*. Reprinted by permission of Eyre Methuen Ltd. as British publishers and Grove Press, Inc.

James Joyce: Extract from *Ulysses*. Copyright 1914, 1918 by Margaret Caroline Anderson and renewed 1942, 1946 by Nora

ACKNOWLEDGEMENTS

Joseph Joyce. Reprinted by permission of The Bodley Head Ltd. The Society of Authors as the literary representative of the Estate of James Joyce, and Random House, Inc.

Rudyard Kipling: Extract from *Something of Myself*. Reprinted by permission of A. P. Watt Ltd.

T. E. Lawrence: Extract from *The Letters of T. E. Lawrence of Arabia*, edited by David Garnett. Reprinted by permission of Jonathan Cape Ltd. on behalf of the editor and the Letters of T. E. Lawrence Trust.

Laurie Lee: Extract from *Cider with Rosie*. Reprinted by permission of the Hogarth Press, Ltd.

Rose Macaulay: Extract from *Told by an Idiot* (Collins, 1928). Reprinted by permission of A. D. Peters & Co. Ltd.

Cyra McFadden: From *The Serial*. Copyright © 1976, 1977 by Cyra McFadden. Reprinted by permission of Alfred A. Knopf Inc. and Elaine Markson Literary Agency, Inc.

Compton MacKenzie: Extract from *My Life and Times*. Reprinted by permission of Chatto and Windus for the Author's Literary Estate.

Louis MacNeice: From *Selected Poems* (Faber). Reprinted by permission of David Higham Associates Ltd.

W. Somerset Maugham: Extract from *Cakes and Ale*. Reprinted by permission of A. P. Watt Ltd.

A. A. Milne: Extract from *It's Too Late Now*. Copyright 1939 by A. A. Milne, copyright renewal © 1967 by Daphne Milne. Reprinted by kind permission of Curtis Brown Ltd.

Iris Murdoch: Extract from *The Red and the Green*. Copyright © 1965 by Iris Murdoch. Reprinted by permission of Chatto & Windus Ltd. and Viking Penguin Inc.

Bernard Newman: Extract from *Speaking from Memory*. Reprinted by permission of Anthony Sheil Associates.

New Yorker: Extract from 'Notes and Comment' from *The Talk of the Town*, in the *New Yorker*, 11 July 1977. Copyright © 1977 The New Yorker Magazine, Inc. Reprinted by permission.

Leslie Norris: Extract from *Sliding*. Copyright © 1976 by Leslie Norris. Reprinted by permission of J. M. Dent & Sons Ltd., and Brandt & Brandt, Inc., New York. Extract from 'A Small War' from *Mountains Polecats Pheasants*. Reprinted by permission of Chatto & Windus Ltd.

Flann O'Brien: Extracts from *The Third Policeman*. Reprinted by permission of Granada Publishing Ltd., and A. M. Heath & Co. Ltd. for the estate of the late Flann O'Brien.

Thomas Pakenham: Extract from *The Boer War*. Reprinted by permission of George Weidenfeld & Nicolson Ltd. & Curtis Brown Ltd.

J. B. Priestley: Extract from *The English Journey*. Reprinted by permission of Wm. Heinemann Ltd.

ACKNOWLEDGEMENTS

Gwen Raverat: Extracts from *Period Piece*. Reprinted by permission of Faber & Faber Ltd.

Dorothy Richardson: Extract from *Pilgrimage*. Reprinted by permission of Virago Ltd.

Bertrand Russell: Extract from *Autobiography of Bertrand Russell*. Reprinted by permission of George Allen & Unwin (Publ.) Ltd. Extract from *Portraits from Memory*. Reprinted by permission of George Allen & Unwin (Publ.) Ltd. and Simon & Schuster, New York.

Viscount Samuel: Extract from *Memoirs* (Cresset Press, 1945).

William Saroyan: Extract from *The Bicycle Rider in Beverley Hills*. Reprinted by permission of Laurence Pollinger Ltd.

George Bernard Shaw: Extracts from letters 1895 & 1897 from *Collected Letters of G. B. Shaw* (ed. Dan Lawrence, Reinhardt, 1965). Reprinted by permission of The Society of Authors on behalf of the Bernard Shaw Estate.

Alan Sillitoe: Extracts from *Saturday Night and Sunday Morning*. Reprinted by permission of W. H. Allen & Co. Ltd. Extract from 'The Bike' (first published in *The Ragman's Daughter*, W. H. Allen, 1963). Reprinted by permission of Rosica Colin Ltd.

Robert Speaight: Extract from *Hilaire Belloc*. Reprinted by permission of A. D. Peters & Co. Ltd.

Flora Thompson: Extract from *Candleford Green* from *Lark Rise to Candleford* (1954). Reprinted by permission of Oxford University Press.

Calvin Tomkins: Extract from *The Bride and the Bachelors*. Copyright © 1962, 1964, 1965 by Calvin Tomkins. Reprinted by permission of George Weidenfeld & Nicolson Ltd. and Viking Penguin, Inc.

G. M. Trevelyan: Extract from *An Autobiography*. Reprinted by permission of the Longman Group Ltd.

John Wain: Extract from *Hurry on Down*. Reprinted by permission of Secker & Warburg Ltd. and Curtis Brown Ltd.

H. G. Wells: Extracts from *The Wheels of Chance*, *The History of Mr. Polly*, and *Experiment in Autobiography*. Reprinted by permission of A. P. Watt Ltd.

Emlyn Williams: Extract from *George: An Early Autobiography*. Copyright © 1961 by Emlyn Williams. Reprinted by permission of Hamish Hamilton Ltd. and Random House, Inc.

Ronald Williams: Extract from 'De Motu Urbanorum', in *British Medical Journal*, 4 October 1975. Reprinted by permission of the author.

P. G. Wodehouse: Extract from *Carry on Jeeves*. Reprinted by permission of A. P. Watt Ltd.

Leonard Woolf: Extract from *Sowing*. Copyright © 1960 by Leonard Woolf. Reprinted by permission of The Hogarth

ACKNOWLEDGEMENTS

Press for The Author's Literary Estate, and Harcourt Brace
Jovanovich, Inc.

Yevgeny Yevtushenko: Extract from 'On a Bicycle' from Yevtushenko: *Selected Poems* trans. Robin Milner-Gulland and Peter
Levi (Penguin Modern European Poets, 1962), p. 61. Copyright
© Robin Milner-Gulland and Peter Levi 1962. Reprinted by
permission of Penguin Books Ltd.

While every effort has been made to secure permission, we may
have failed in a few cases to trace the copyright holder. We
apologize for any apparent negligence.

The illustrations in this book were taken from the following
sources: Earl of Albemarle and G. Lacy Hillier, *Cycling* (London,
1895); *Harper's* (1869); O. Jennings, *La Santé par le Tricycle*
(Paris, 1889); Zucker, *A Source Book of Early French Advertising
Art* (London, 1970).

Index of Authors

Anon, 3, 11, 28
Anthony, Michael, 86–7
Auden, W. H., 80–1

Balfour, A. J., 60
Bates, H. E., 83–4
Beckett, Samuel, 100
Bee, 21
Beeching, Henry C., 34, 38–9
Beerbohm, Max, 32
Belloc, Hilaire, 12
Bennett, Arnold, 6–7, 55–6
Bernstein, Carl, 98
Betjeman, Sir John, 66, 70–1, 77, 79
Bicycling News, 13
Blackwoods Magazine, 2
Blatchford, Robert, 37
Boas, Guy, 91
Boswell, James, 1
Boylan, Grace Duff, 26
Brayne, Mark, 90

Cambridge University Bicycle Club, 11
Church, Richard, 15–16, 39, 48–50
Columbiad. The, 9
Croft-Cooke, R., 97
Cummings, Peter, 78
Cycling, 10
Cycling Magazine, 33

Dacre, Harry, 47–8
Day-Lewis, Cecil, 70
Doyle, Sir Arthur Conan, 44–5
Duchamp, Marcel, 99

Empson, William, 84
English Mechanic, 7

Fitzgerald, F. Scott, 47
Flagg, J. M., 24

Gaulois, Le, 4
Gilbert, W. S., 32
Girl of the Period Miscellany, 3
Gissing, George, 58
Gladstone, William Ewart, 60
Graves, Robert, 89, 100
Grey, Lord Edward, 61
Gunn, Neil, 74–5

Hardy, Thomas, 59
Hartley, L. P., 66–7
Hawker, James, 11–12
Herbert, Revd. G., 6
Holmes, Oliver Wendell, 3
Hub, The, 15
Hudson, W. H., 37–8, 43
Hurne. Richard, 87–8

Illitch, Ivan, 84, 94

James, Henry, 58
Jarry, Alfred, 89
Jerome, Jerome K., 27, 29, 39–41
Jersey, Countess of, 61–2
Joyce, James, 96

Keats, John, 1
Kendall, Walter G., 36
Kipling, Rudyard, 59

Lawrence, D. H., 80
Lawrence, T. E., 77–8
Lee, Laurie, 30

Macaulay, Rose, 18, 33
McFadden, Cyra, 98
MacKenzie, Compton, 23, 69
MacNeice, Louis, 71–2
Maugham, W. Somerset, 67–8
Maurice, Maj.-Gen. F., 64
Milne, A. A., 48, 68
Milner, Alfred, 62–3
Morning Chronicle, 2

[109]